World War II Stories for Kids

15 Inspirational Tales of the Greatest Battles,

Best Leaders, and Heroic Moments

Spencer Pickens

Table of Contents

CHAPTER 1:

The Battle of Britain: The Air War for England

In the summer of 1940, the skies above England became the stage for one of the most significant battles of World War II: the Battle of Britain. This wasn't just any battle; it was the first major campaign to be fought entirely by air forces. The stakes were high, and the outcome would determine the fate of Britain and possibly the entire war.

The main characters in this aerial drama were the brave pilots of the Royal Air Force (RAF), who faced the formidable German Luftwaffe. The RAF pilots were a diverse group, coming from all walks of life and even different countries, but they shared a common goal: to defend their homeland from invasion.

One of these pilots was a young man named Edward. Edward had always dreamed of flying, and when the war broke out, he saw it as his duty to join the RAF. He knew the risks involved but believed in fighting for freedom against tyranny.

As Edward climbed into his Spitfire, the iconic fighter plane of the RAF, he felt a mix of excitement and fear. The Spitfire was a marvel of engineering, fast and maneuverable, but he knew that skill and courage would be just as important as the machine he piloted.

The Battle of Britain was not just a single event but a series of attacks that lasted for months. The German Luftwaffe, confident from their successes in mainland Europe, aimed to destroy the RAF and gain air superiority over England. This would pave the way for an invasion. Their plan was to bomb RAF airfields, radar stations, and later, cities and civilian targets in a campaign of terror.

The first major attacks began in July 1940, with the Luftwaffe targeting coastal shipping convoys and ports. Edward and his fellow pilots were scrambled day after day to meet the enemy in the skies. The fighting was intense, with dogfights occurring at breakneck speeds high above the ground. Pilots had to be alert every second, knowing that a single mistake could be fatal.

Despite the danger, there was a sense of camaraderie among the pilots. They relied on each other for support, both in the air and on the ground. After each mission, they would gather to share stories of narrow escapes and victories, always aware that some seats might be empty the next day.

The statistics of the battle were staggering. At its height, the Luftwaffe could muster over 2,500 aircraft, including fighters and bombers. In contrast, the RAF had around 640 fighters available for defense. The odds seemed overwhelming, but the RAF had two secret weapons: the Spitfire and the Hurricane fighters, both superior in performance to much of the Luftwaffe's fleet, and the newly developed radar technology that allowed them to detect incoming attacks.

This technological edge, combined with the bravery and skill of pilots like Edward, allowed the RAF to meet the German attacks with surprising effectiveness. Each day brought intense aerial combat, with both sides suffering losses. But the spirit of the British pilots never waned; they knew they were fighting not just for their own survival but for the freedom of their country.

As Edward took to the skies on another mission, he thought of his family and friends below, going about their lives under the constant threat of bombing raids. He flew not just as a pilot of the RAF but as a protector of his homeland, determined to keep the skies of Britain free from invasion. The Battle of Britain was a test of wills, and Edward, like so many others, was resolved to do whatever it took to emerge victorious.

The Battle of Britain intensified as the summer of 1940 wore on. Edward and his fellow RAF pilots faced relentless sorties, sometimes flying multiple missions in a single day. The strain on both pilots and aircraft was immense, but the resolve of the RAF remained unbroken. They were determined to protect their country against the might of the Luftwaffe, which was launching attacks in ever-increasing numbers.

3

As August began, the Luftwaffe shifted its focus, launching all-out attacks on RAF airfields and radar stations. The strategy was clear: destroy the RAF's ability to fight and clear the way for Operation Sea Lion, the planned German invasion of Britain. Edward found himself flying to defend airbases one day, and radar stations the next, the importance of which could not be overstated. These radar stations were the eyes of Britain, providing early warning of incoming German raids.

One particular day stood out in Edward's memory. He had been scrambled to intercept a large formation of German bombers, escorted by fighters, heading towards an important radar station on the southern coast. As he and his squadron engaged the enemy, Edward realized the stakes were higher than ever. Losing the radar station would blind the RAF, making it nearly impossible to effectively counter German attacks.

The dogfight was chaotic. Edward's Spitfire danced through the sky, twisting and turning as he chased down German bombers and evaded their escorts. The sky was filled with aircraft, contrails, and the deadly ballet of aerial combat. Despite the danger, Edward felt alive, every sense heightened as he pushed himself and his aircraft to the limit.

The battle for the radar station was fierce but ultimately successful. Edward's squadron managed to down several German bombers and drive off the escorts. The radar station remained operational, a crucial victory for the RAF. The significance of this win was not lost on Edward or his comrades; they knew they had protected a vital asset in the defense of Britain.

The courage and skill of RAF pilots like Edward were making a difference, but the cost was high. The toll of continuous combat was evident in the fatigue that settled over the pilots and the losses they endured. Every mission could be their last, a reality they lived with daily. Yet, their spirit remained indomitable, bolstered by the support of the British public and the clear knowledge that they were the last line of defense against invasion.

The Luftwaffe's strategy also included terror bombing raids on British cities, intended to break the will of the British people. This phase of the battle, known as the Blitz, saw cities across Britain, including London, subjected to nightly bombing raids. The devastation was widespread, but rather than breaking the British spirit, it only strengthened their resolve to resist.

Edward and his squadron were often called upon to intercept these bombers, a task that took them over the burning cities of Britain. Flying above London at night, amidst the anti-aircraft fire and the glow of fires below, was a surreal experience. It underscored the stakes of their fight, not just for military victory but for the lives and freedom of their fellow citizens.

The Battle of Britain was not just a military conflict; it was a testament to the resilience of the British people and the bravery of the RAF. The pilots, ground crew, and civilians each played a crucial role in this historic battle. For Edward and his fellow pilots, the sky above Britain was more than just a battlefield; it was the front line in the fight for freedom, a cause they believed in deeply and were willing to sacrifice everything for.

As the summer turned to autumn, the battle continued, but the resolve of the RAF and the British people remained unshaken. Edward, flying sortie after sortie, felt a deep connection to his country and its people, a bond forged in the fires of conflict. The Battle of Britain would prove to be a turning point in the war, a moment when the tide began to turn against the Axis powers, thanks in no small part to the courage of the few, of whom Edward was proudly one.

As the Battle of Britain raged through the autumn of 1940, Edward and the RAF faced new challenges. The German Luftwaffe, frustrated by their inability to gain air superiority, began to change tactics. Their targets expanded, and the intensity of their attacks increased. For Edward, this meant not only defending the strategic sites but also flying over cities, protecting civilians from the terror of the bombings.

One crisp October day, Edward's squadron received orders for a mission that would remain etched in his memory forever. A large formation of German bombers, escorted by fighters, was heading towards London, intent on unleashing destruction upon the historic city. The RAF's mission was clear: stop the bombers at all costs.

As they took to the skies, Edward felt a mix of determination and apprehension. London was more than just a city; it was the heart of Britain, symbolizing the nation's resilience and resolve. The thought of it under attack was personal, not just for Edward but for every pilot in the squadron.

The engagement that followed was among the most intense Edward had experienced. The Luftwaffe had sent one of its largest formations yet, and the skies over London became a furious battleground. Edward found himself in a relentless dogfight, maneuvering his Spitfire with precision, diving and climbing as he pursued his targets.

Despite the overwhelming odds, Edward and his squadron fought valiantly, their actions guided by a deep sense of duty. They knew that each German bomber they downed was saving lives on the ground, preventing the destruction of homes and historic landmarks. The battle was fierce, but the pilots of the RAF were fiercer, embodying the spirit of the famous Winston Churchill speech where he declared, "Never in the field of human conflict was so much owed by so many to so few."

The aftermath of the battle was a testament to the courage of Edward and his fellow pilots. London had withstood the attack, and while the damage was significant, the spirit of the city and its people remained unbroken. The pilots returned to their base, weary but aware that their efforts had made a difference.

In the days that followed, Edward noticed a change in the atmosphere among the pilots and the British people. There was a sense of solidarity, a shared understanding that they were all in this together, fighting for the very soul of Britain. The Battle of Britain had become more than a military engagement; it was a symbol of resistance, a declaration that Britain would never surrender.

The statistics of the battle were sobering. Over the course of several months, the RAF lost more than 1,000 aircraft, and many brave pilots lost their lives or were injured. The Luftwaffe's losses were even higher, which significantly weakened their ability to carry out future operations. The battle had exacted a heavy toll, but it had also proven the effectiveness and resilience of the RAF.

For Edward, the Battle of Britain was a defining period in his life. It had tested his limits, taught him the value of teamwork and sacrifice, and shown him the depths of human courage. He had flown with some of the best pilots in the world, defending his country against a formidable enemy. The experience would stay with him forever, shaping him as a pilot and a person.

The Battle of Britain ended with no clear victory for the Luftwaffe, marking a turning point in World War II. Britain had stood firm against the might of Hitler's forces, thanks in large part to the efforts of the RAF. The battle had demonstrated that air power could be decisive in modern warfare and that the spirit of a nation could be its most powerful weapon.

Edward's story is but one of many, each contributing to the tapestry of history that defines the battle. It's a story of triumph against the odds, a testament to the power of unity and determination in the face of adversity.

CHAPTER 2:

Winston Churchill: The Voice of Victory

In the heart of London, amidst the turmoil of World War II, stood a man whose words would become a beacon of hope and resilience for a nation under siege. This man was Winston Churchill, the Prime Minister of the United Kingdom. Known for his indomitable spirit and stirring oratory, Churchill's speeches during the war years would inspire not just the British people but generations to come.

Churchill became Prime Minister on May 10, 1940, at a time when the shadows of war loomed large over Europe. Britain stood alone against the might of Nazi Germany, which had already conquered much of the continent. The situation was dire, with many fearing that Britain would be the next to fall. But Churchill was not a man to be easily daunted.

From the moment he took office, Churchill knew that his words had the power to uplift the spirits of his fellow countrymen.

He was not just leading a country; he was rallying a nation to stand firm against tyranny. One of his first actions as Prime Minister was to address the House of Commons, delivering a speech that would be remembered for its courage and defiance.

"We have before us an ordeal of the most grievous kind. We have before us many, many long months of struggle and of suffering," Churchill declared. Yet, his speech was not one of despair but of determination. "You ask, what is our policy? I will say it is to wage war, by sea, land, and air, with all our might and with all the strength that God can give us; to wage war against a monstrous tyranny, never surpassed in the dark, lamentable catalogue of human crime. This is our policy. You ask, what is our aim? I can answer in one word: Victory. Victory at all costs, Victory in spite of all terror, Victory, however long and hard the road may be; for without victory, there is no survival."

Churchill's words struck a chord with the British people. His refusal to consider defeat, his belief in victory, and his resolve to fight on gave hope to a nation facing its darkest hour. It was a call to arms, an invocation of the British spirit of endurance and resilience.

In the weeks and months that followed, Churchill's speeches became a vital part of the British war effort. He spoke not only to inform but to inspire. Each broadcast was an opportunity to reassure the public, to bolster their spirits, and to remind them of what they were fighting for.

One of Churchill's most famous speeches was delivered on

June 18, 1940, after the fall of France. With Europe overrun by the Nazis and Britain vulnerable to invasion, Churchill addressed the nation. "The Battle of France is over. The Battle of Britain is about to begin," he announced. Then came the words that would echo through history: "Let us therefore brace ourselves to our duties, and so bear ourselves that, if the British Empire and its Commonwealth last for a thousand years, men will still say, 'This was their finest hour.'"

This speech did more than rally the British people; it defined them. Churchill's "finest hour" speech encapsulated the spirit of defiance and determination that would characterize the British resistance throughout the war. It was a declaration that Britain would not bend, would not break, and would fight on to victory, no matter the cost.

Understanding Churchill's role provides a powerful lesson in the importance of words and the strength of will. Through his speeches, Churchill was not just communicating; he was leading. He transformed his personal conviction into a collective resolve, uniting a nation with the power of his voice.

Winston Churchill's leadership during World War II wasn't just about his powerful speeches; it was also about the decisions he made and the strategies he employed to navigate Britain through its most perilous times. However, Churchill knew that to keep the nation's morale high, he needed to communicate effectively, blending realism with hope, and always aiming to inspire confidence in victory.

In the midst of the Blitz, when German bombers turned night skies into a canvas of fire over British cities, Churchill's voice continued to resonate, offering solace and strength to those huddled in bomb shelters and those fighting on the front lines. His visits to bombed-out neighborhoods and his appearances in places where the war's scars were most visible were not just acts of leadership; they were symbols of shared resolve and common purpose. Churchill didn't stand above the conflict; he stood within it, alongside his fellow Britons.

One particularly impactful moment came after Churchill visited the east end of London, an area heavily damaged by the Blitz. The imagery of Churchill, hat in hand, surveying the damage and speaking directly with the people affected, became a powerful symbol of unity and resilience. "We can take it!" became a rallying cry, encapsulating the British determination to withstand the bombings and keep fighting.

Churchill's leadership was characterized by his ability to see beyond the immediate crisis to the broader context of the war. He was instrumental in forging alliances, most notably with the United States and the Soviet Union, understanding early on that victory in a global conflict would require global cooperation. His relationship with U.S. President Franklin D. Roosevelt was particularly significant, leading to the Atlantic Charter, which outlined the vision for a post-war world even as the conflict raged on.

Despite the gravity of his role, Churchill was known for his wit and his ability to use humor as a tool for both lifting spirits and cutting through diplomatic niceties. His quips and speeches often contained memorable lines that not only made headlines but also made the immense challenges of the war seem more bearable. For instance, in addressing the threat of invasion, Churchill humorously remarked, "We shall fight on the beaches, we shall fight on the landing grounds, we shall fight in the fields and in the streets, we shall fight in the hills; we shall never surrender." His humor was not frivolous but strategic, a means of humanizing the conflict and making the national effort more relatable.

Churchill's speeches and radio broadcasts were carefully crafted to reach every corner of the British Isles, ensuring that his message of perseverance and unity was heard by all. The statistics from this period reveal the scale of the challenge Britain faced: hundreds of thousands of homes destroyed, millions of lives disrupted, and a constant threat of invasion. Yet, through it all, Churchill's words helped to weave a narrative of endurance and defiance that kept the British spirit alive.

Churchill's leadership offers a lesson in the power of words to inspire action and instill courage. His speeches were not just messages of hope; they were instruments of leadership, guiding a nation through its darkest hours with the promise of a brighter future. As we continue to explore Churchill's impact on World War II, it becomes clear that his voice was not just the voice of victory; it was the voice of a nation united in the face of adversity, determined to stand firm and fight on until the end.

While Winston Churchill's speeches provided inspiration and

strength to the British people and the Allied forces, his leadership was also defined by his relentless energy and involvement in the war effort. Churchill was not one to lead from the sidelines; he immersed himself in the details of military strategy and was often found in the war rooms, discussing plans with his generals and advisors. His hands-on approach was a testament to his commitment to victory and his willingness to shoulder the heavy burden of command.

Churchill's influence extended beyond the boundaries of Britain. Recognizing the importance of a united front against the Axis powers, he worked tirelessly to strengthen ties with Allied nations. His travels to meet with other world leaders, such as his meetings with President Roosevelt and Soviet leader Joseph Stalin, were crucial in coordinating the military and political efforts necessary to defeat Nazi Germany and its allies. These high-stakes meetings involved complex negotiations and strategic planning, with Churchill often playing a key role in bridging differences and forging a path forward.

Despite the immense pressures of leading a nation at war, Churchill was known for his ability to maintain a sense of balance. He understood the importance of rest and relaxation for sustaining one's energy and spirit. Stories of Churchill taking brief naps during the day or painting to relieve stress highlight a leader who knew the value of self-care, even in the midst of global conflict. These personal habits were part of what made him resilient, allowing him to navigate the ups and downs of the war with unwavering determination.

Churchill was not without his criticisms. There were moments of doubt and debate among the British public and within the government about certain decisions and strategies. However, Churchill's ability to communicate his vision and rationale, coupled with his evident dedication to the cause, often helped to quell concerns and rally support. His belief in victory, even in the face of setbacks, served as a guiding light for the nation.

The impact of Churchill's leadership during World War II cannot be overstated. His speeches and actions helped to shape the course of the war and the destiny of the free world. For children learning about this period, Churchill's story is an example of how determination, courage, and the power of communication can influence history. His legacy teaches us that leadership involves not just guiding others but inspiring them to achieve their collective potential.

As the war progressed, Churchill's vision of a post-war world began to take shape. He was instrumental in laying the groundwork for the United Nations and advocating for peace and stability in the aftermath of the conflict. His foresight in these matters demonstrated a leader who was not only focused on winning the war but also on building a lasting peace.

Churchill's voice of victory was more than just rhetoric; it was a manifestation of his leadership style, marked by resilience, strategic thinking, and an unwavering commitment to freedom and democracy. His speeches continue to inspire, reminding us of the enduring power of words to uplift and motivate, even in the face of the greatest challenges. As this chapter on Winston Churchill draws to a close, readers are left with a deeper understanding of the man whose leadership helped to steer the course of history and secure a brighter future for generations to come.

CHAPTER 3:

Awakening the Sleeping Giant: America Enters the War

On a peaceful Sunday morning, December 7, 1941, the sky above Pearl Harbor, a beautiful naval base located in Hawaii, was as blue as the ocean that cradled the ships of the United States Pacific Fleet. The sailors, enjoying a rare day of rest, had no idea that their lives and the course of history were about to change forever.

The first wave of Japanese airplanes struck at 7:55 a.m., catching the American naval base almost entirely off guard. The attackers, aiming to cripple the U.S. Pacific Fleet, targeted battleships and airfields with bombs, torpedoes, and machine-gun fire. Explosions and gunfire quickly turned the serene morning into chaos. Sailors and soldiers rushed to their battle stations, while pilots attempted to get their planes off the ground amidst the onslaught.

One of the most tragic losses of the day was the sinking of the USS Arizona. A bomb detonated the ship's ammunition magazine, causing a massive explosion that sank the battleship within minutes, trapping hundreds of men inside. Nearby, the USS Oklahoma capsized, trapping its crew as well. In total, 12 ships were sunk or beached, and 9 were damaged.

Airfields were also a major target of the attack. Rows of American planes, lined up wingtip to wingtip, became easy targets. The destruction of aircraft on the ground ensured that American forces were unable to mount a significant counterattack during the initial stages of the assault.

As the second wave of Japanese planes arrived, the situation grew even more desperate. However, American anti-aircraft fire began to take a toll on the attackers, shooting down several enemy aircraft. Amid the devastation, acts of heroism emerged. Men like Lieutenant John Finn manned machine guns, firing at the incoming planes, despite being wounded multiple times.

In just over two hours, the attack was over, leaving 2,403 Americans dead and 1,178 wounded. The Pacific Fleet appeared to be crippled, with eight battleships out of action. However, the Japanese had failed to destroy important oil storage facilities, submarine bases, and, most crucially, the American aircraft carriers, which were not in port that day.

The attack on Pearl Harbor shocked the American public and led directly to the United States' entry into World War II. President Franklin D. Roosevelt addressed Congress on December 8, calling for a declaration of war against Japan, describing the previous day as "a date which will live in infamy." This moment galvanized the American people, uniting them in a common cause to fight against the Axis powers.

In the aftermath, the United States mobilized for war on an unprecedented scale. The attack on Pearl Harbor, while a tragic loss, awakened the "sleeping giant" of American industrial and military might. The nation's response would eventually turn the tide of the war in the Allies' favor

Through the story of Pearl Harbor, we can learn about the impact of unexpected events on the course of history, the resilience in the face of adversity, and the importance of unity and determination in overcoming challenges.

The attack on Pearl Harbor marked a pivotal moment in world history, drawing the United States into World War II, a conflict that had been raging across Europe and Asia. The strategic aim of the Japanese was to neutralize the U.S. Pacific Fleet, ensuring Japan could advance its territorial ambitions in Southeast Asia and the Pacific without interference. This attack was intended to be a devastating blow to American military capacity, specifically targeting the battleships moored at Pearl Harbor, as battleships were considered crucial to naval power at the time.

In the wake of the attack, the United States faced significant losses. The sinking of the USS Arizona became a symbol of the day's tragedy, with 1,177 crew members losing their lives when the battleship exploded and sank. The overall toll was harrowing, with

2,403 Americans killed and over a thousand wounded. The material damage was also severe, with multiple ships sunk or damaged and hundreds of aircraft destroyed or incapacitated.

However, the attack did not achieve all its strategic objectives. Crucially, the U.S. Navy's aircraft carriers were not in port during the attack and thus escaped damage. These carriers would play a pivotal role in the Pacific Theater, contributing to key victories at battles such as Midway, which shifted the momentum of the war in the Allies' favor.

The immediate aftermath of Pearl Harbor saw a united American response. The country, previously divided over the issue of entering the war, came together with a shared purpose. President Franklin D. Roosevelt's declaration that December 7, 1941, was "a date which will live in infamy," captured the national mood, and his request for a declaration of war against Japan was met with near-unanimous approval from Congress. Subsequently, declarations of war between the United States and the Axis powers of Germany and Italy solidified the U.S.'s involvement in World War II.

The attack on Pearl Harbor had far-reaching implications beyond its immediate military impact. It galvanized American industrial and military mobilization, leading to an unprecedented wartime effort that would play a crucial role in the Allied victory. The event also marked a turning point in how warfare was conducted, highlighting the increasing importance of naval air power and leading to changes in military strategy and tactics.

The story of Pearl Harbor is not just one of loss and tragedy but also resilience and unity. It serves as a reminder of the costs of war, the importance of preparedness, and the strength that can emerge from adversity. The lessons learned from Pearl Harbor continue to resonate, underscoring the need for vigilance, diplomacy, and a commitment to peace.

In the chaos of the attack, countless service members and civilians worked with extraordinary courage to save lives, even at great risk to their own. Nurses, doctors, and medics provided urgent care under dire conditions, treating burns, shrapnel wounds, and other severe injuries caused by the bombings and gunfire. Amidst the devastation, their efforts were a beacon of hope and humanity.

Firefighters and rescue workers rushed to contain fires on ships and buildings, often navigating through smoke, oil-slicked water, and debris. Their swift actions prevented further loss of life and damage, showcasing the critical role of first responders in times of crisis.

Sailors trapped in sinking ships fought to survive and aid their fellow crewmembers. Stories of survival and escape from the USS Arizona, USS Oklahoma, and other stricken vessels speak to the chaos and desperation of the moment, but also to the incredible will to live and the solidarity among those caught in the attack.

Amidst the defense efforts, anti-aircraft gunners, many of whom were young servicemen, manned their weapons to return fire against the attacking planes. Their actions downed several Japanese aircraft, marking the beginning of America's military response to the attack.

The story of Pearl Harbor also highlights the role of intelligence and preparedness in national defense. In the aftermath, investigations and reflections on the attack underscored the importance of vigilance, communication, and readiness to respond to threats. The lessons learned from Pearl Harbor influenced military and governmental policies and procedures to prevent future surprises of a similar nature.

Understanding the attack on Pearl Harbor involves recognizing the complexities of global politics, the impacts of war, and the profound resilience of individuals in the face of adversity. It's a chapter in history that illustrates the cost of conflict, the value of peace, and the enduring spirit of a nation to overcome challenges and emerge stronger.

As we reflect on Pearl Harbor, it's essential to remember both the pain of loss and the strength of the human spirit. The attack galvanized the United States, leading to significant contributions to the Allied victory in World War II. It's a reminder of the sacrifices made by those who serve and the importance of working towards a world where peace and security prevail for all.

CHAPTER 4:

The Battle of Midway: Under the Pacific Sun

In the vast expanse of the Pacific Ocean, under the blazing sun, a pivotal moment in World War II unfolded. This was the Battle of Midway, a confrontation that would become known as one of the most significant naval battles in history. Taking place between June 4th and June 7th, 1942, just six months after the attack on Pearl Harbor, Midway was a battle of wits, strategy, and courage.

At the heart of this story were the sailors and pilots from both the United States and Japan, each determined to serve their country. Among them was a young American pilot named Tom. Tom had joined the Navy with a burning desire to make a difference, and now, above the waters of Midway Atoll, he would get his chance.

The United States had been on high alert since Pearl Harbor. The Japanese navy, confident after their successes in Asia and the

Pacific, planned to lure the American fleet into a trap at Midway, hoping to destroy it once and for all. What the Japanese didn't know was that American codebreakers had cracked their secret communications, giving the U.S. Navy a critical advantage: foreknowledge of the Japanese plans.

As the sun rose on June 4th, the sea and sky around Midway became a battlefield. Tom, piloting one of the torpedo bombers, felt both the weight of responsibility and the thrill of the challenge. His mission was to attack the Japanese aircraft carriers, the heart of their fleet. The task was daunting; the bombers would have to fly through a hail of enemy fire to reach their targets.

The Japanese fleet was formidable, boasting four aircraft carriers, along with a host of battleships and cruisers. In contrast, the United States had three carriers at Midway, but what they lacked in numbers, they made up for in determination and strategy.

The first day of the battle was intense. American bombers, including Tom's squadron, took to the air, facing fierce resistance from Japanese fighter planes. The skies were filled with the roar of engines and the crackle of gunfire. Despite the danger, Tom and his fellow pilots pressed on, knowing the fate of the battle and perhaps the war in the Pacific rested in their hands.

On the ocean below, ships maneuvered for position, launching aircraft and exchanging volleys of fire. The commanders of both fleets knew the importance of this battle; Midway was not just a strategic point on the map but a symbol of control in the Pacific.

The Americans faced setbacks early on. The Japanese air defenses were strong, and several American bombers were lost without reaching their targets. However, perseverance was a trait the American forces had in abundance. Wave after wave of bombers took off from the carriers, each pilot determined to play their part in the fight.

Tom's squadron finally saw their opportunity. Diving through enemy fire, they released their torpedoes at one of the Japanese carriers. The moments that followed seemed to stretch into eternity as they awaited the impact. Then, a direct hit. One of the enemy carriers was engulfed in flames, a critical blow to the Japanese fleet.

The success was hard-won, and the battle was far from over. As Tom's plane limped back to the carrier, low on fuel and with one engine damaged, he knew that the coming days would test them all like never before. But for now, there was a glimmer of hope. The Battle of Midway was proving to be a turning point, not just in the war in the Pacific, but in the confidence and resolve of the American forces.

As we follow Tom's journey through the Battle of Midway, they witness the courage and resilience required in times of war. They learn about the importance of intelligence, strategy, and the sheer will to overcome seemingly insurmountable odds. The Battle of Midway, under the relentless Pacific sun, was more than a clash of fleets; it was a testament to the human spirit's capacity for bravery and perseverance in the face of adversity.

The dawn of June 5th brought a renewed sense of purpose

25

among the American forces. The victory from the previous day had bolstered their spirits, but everyone knew that the battle was far from over. Tom, despite the fatigue that clung to his bones and the vivid memories of the previous day's dogfights, prepared himself for another sortie. The American commanders were keen to press their advantage, understanding that the element of surprise was now squarely on their side.

As Tom and his fellow pilots took to the skies, the ocean below was a chessboard of ships maneuvering for position. The Japanese fleet, taken aback by the loss of one of their carriers, was now more cautious, but no less determined to seize control of Midway and cripple the American naval power in the Pacific.

The battle strategy for the Americans was clear: target the remaining Japanese carriers. Aircraft carriers were the backbone of naval power in the Pacific, serving as floating airbases that could project force far beyond the range of traditional battleships. If the United States could neutralize Japan's carriers, they could shift the balance of power in the Pacific.

Tom's bomber squadron was tasked with a daring mission: to find and attack the Japanese carrier Akagi. The Akagi was not just any ship; it was a flagship of the Japanese fleet, carrying some of the most experienced pilots and crew. Approaching the Akagi would mean running a gauntlet of enemy fighters and anti-aircraft fire.

As they approached their target, the tension among Tom and his squadron was palpable. They flew low, skimming the waves to avoid detection for as long as possible. Suddenly, the Akagi loomed before them, a giant of steel and menace. Tom's heart pounded as he lined up for his bombing run. Flak exploded all around, filling the air with deadly shrapnel. Japanese Zero fighters darted towards them, guns blazing.

In that moment, Tom's training took over. He focused on his target, releasing his bombs at just the right moment before pulling up in a steep climb to avoid the blast. The seconds stretched out as he waited to see if his attack had been successful. Then, confirmation came over the radio: the bombs had hit their mark. The Akagi was severely damaged, its flight deck ablaze, a significant victory for the American forces.

Back on the American carriers, the mood was cautiously optimistic. The pilots and crew knew that the battle was turning in their favor, but the cost was high. Many planes did not return, and those that did were often riddled with bullet holes or carrying injured crew members. The sacrifice of these brave individuals was not lost on Tom or his comrades. Each mission was a reminder of the price of freedom and the harsh realities of war.

The battle continued through June 6th and into June 7th, with both sides experiencing losses and victories. For the Americans, the focus remained on disabling the Japanese carriers, while the Japanese sought to strike back and regain their lost momentum. The skies above Midway and the surrounding ocean were a constant churn of aircraft and naval vessels engaged in a dance of death and survival.

Throughout it all, Tom flew mission after mission, each time pushing himself and his aircraft to the limit. The Battle of Midway was not just a test of military might; it was a test of wills, a confrontation between the desire for conquest and the resolve to defend one's home and values.

As the battle drew to a close, the toll it had taken was evident. The once-pristine ocean was marred by the scars of battle: sunken ships, oil slicks, and debris. Yet, despite the devastation, there was a sense of accomplishment among the American forces. Through their courage and sacrifice, they had turned the tide of the war in the Pacific, proving that determination and strategy could overcome even the most formidable challenges.

As the sun rose on June 7th, the final day of the Battle of Midway, the outcome of this monumental clash was becoming clear. The American forces had inflicted devastating blows to the Japanese fleet, sinking three of their four carriers, a crippling blow from which the Japanese Navy would never fully recover during the war. For Tom and his fellow pilots, the day was filled with a mix of exhaustion and elation; their hard work and bravery had paid off, but the cost had been high.

The Japanese, realizing the severity of their losses, began to withdraw, their hopes of capturing Midway and dominating the Pacific dashed. The United States Navy, once considered underdog in this battle, had proven its mettle. The victory at Midway was not just a turning point in the Pacific Theater; it was a testament to the effectiveness of intelligence, strategy, and the indomitable spirit of the American forces.

For Tom, the battle had been a harrowing experience. Each mission had brought its own dangers, from enemy fighters to the ever-present threat of anti-aircraft fire. He had seen friends not return from their sorties, and had himself faced moments when he thought he might not make it back. But through it all, he had kept flying, kept fighting, because he knew that what they were doing was critical to the war effort.

Statistics from the battle tell a story of intense conflict and strategic triumph. The Japanese lost four aircraft carriers, a heavy cruiser, and hundreds of airplanes, along with their highly trained pilots. The Americans, while also suffering losses, including one aircraft carrier and around 150 aircraft, had achieved a victory that shifted the balance of power in the Pacific. The courage and sacrifice of the pilots and sailors had made a decisive difference.

In the aftermath of Midway, Tom and the others were greeted as heroes. Their actions had not only defended Midway but had also given the Allies a much-needed boost in morale. The battle had shown that the United States could stand up to the might of the Japanese Empire and emerge victorious.

Yet, even as they celebrated, there was an understanding that the war was far from over. Midway was a crucial victory, but many battles lay ahead. Tom and his fellow pilots knew they would be called upon again to defend their country and its ideals. The experience of Midway, with its mix of fear, courage, and camaraderie, would stay with them, a reminder of what they had fought for and what they had achieved.

The story of the Battle of Midway is a powerful example of how determination, skill, and bravery can overcome seemingly insurmountable odds. It's a lesson in the importance of intelligence and strategy in warfare, and a tribute to the individuals who put their lives on the line for their country. The battle under the Pacific sun was more than a military engagement; it was a pivotal moment in World War II, shaping the course of the conflict and the lives of those who participated in it.

CHAPTER 5:

The Great Escape: A Leap for Freedom

Deep in the heart of war-torn Europe, behind the imposing barbed wire of Stalag Luft III, a story of extraordinary bravery and ingenuity unfolded. This was no ordinary prisoner-of-war camp. It housed some of the most determined and clever Allied airmen, who refused to let captivity quench their spirit of freedom. Among them were men like Squadron Leader Roger Bushell, a determined and charismatic leader who would orchestrate one of the most daring escape attempts of World War II: The Great Escape.

Stalag Luft III, located in what is now Żagań, Poland, was designed to be escape-proof. High fences, constant guard patrols, and the seclusion of its location were supposed to ensure that no prisoner could escape. However, the guards hadn't accounted for the ingenuity and determination of the men held within.

The plan for the Great Escape was ambitious. It involved

digging three tunnels, codenamed "Tom," "Dick," and "Harry," deep beneath the prison camp, all leading to freedom beyond the camp's fences. The operation was massive, requiring the coordination of over 600 men, each with a specific role to play, from tunnel diggers to guards, to forgers creating fake documents for the escapees.

Bushell and his team knew the risks were high. Previous escape attempts from Stalag Luft III had ended in failure, and the penalties for being caught were severe. Yet, the desire for freedom and the determination to continue fighting the Axis powers from outside the camp's confines drove them forward.

Digging the tunnels was a monumental task. The prisoners used makeshift tools, from spoons to pieces of metal salvaged from the camp. They worked under the cover of darkness and in total secrecy, to avoid detection by the guards. Disposing of the excavated soil was another challenge, as any sign of disturbance could give away their plan. Ingeniously, the prisoners developed a system of dispersing the soil around the camp, hiding it in their clothing during the day and subtly releasing it, a method that required both bravery and caution.

As the tunnels grew longer, the risks increased. Collapses were frequent, and the diggers often found themselves in precarious situations, risking suffocation. Yet, each setback was met with renewed determination. The spirit of cooperation among the prisoners was a testament to their shared goal: freedom.

Bushell, known for his leadership and resolve, kept the morale high, reminding the men of the importance of their task. This was not just an escape attempt; it was a statement of resistance against their captors and the oppressive regime they represented.

The story of the Great Escape is a lesson in perseverance, teamwork, and the indomitable human spirit. It shows that even in the face of overwhelming odds, a group of determined individuals can achieve the extraordinary.

As the tunnels neared completion, the excitement and anxiety among the prisoners grew. They were about to undertake one of the most daring escapes in history, fully aware of the dangers that lay ahead but driven by the hope of freedom and the chance to return to the fight for liberty. The Great Escape was more than a plan for liberation; it was a testament to the courage and resilience of those who refuse to be bound by tyranny.

As the winter of 1943 turned into the early months of 1944, the tunnel known as "Harry" neared completion. Of the three tunnels started, Harry was now the focus of the escape effort, the others having been abandoned or discovered. The air in the camp was thick with tension and anticipation; every man involved knew that their chance to dash for freedom was close at hand.

The tunnel was a marvel of makeshift engineering. Lined with wood scavenged from all corners of the camp, including bed frames, it stretched over 100 meters from beneath the prisoners' barracks to just beyond the camp's perimeter fence. Air was pumped down through a series of pipes made from condensed milk tins, and electric lighting was ingeniously rigged up, powered by the camp's electrical system. It was a testament to the creativity and resilience of the prisoners, who had turned their captivity into an opportunity to outwit their captors.

Squadron Leader Roger Bushell, the mastermind behind the escape plan, knew that timing was everything. The escape was scheduled for a moonless night in late March, to aid the men in staying hidden under the cover of darkness as they made their way across open ground. Each man had been assigned a specific role and time to enter the tunnel, in an effort to avoid detection by the German guards.

On the night of March 24th, 1944, the plan was put into action. The first of the escapees made their way into the tunnel, their hearts racing with a mixture of fear and excitement. The tunnel was cramped and muddy, and progress was slow and arduous. Yet, one by one, the men crawled through to freedom, emerging on the other side to find themselves outside the camp's perimeter.

The plan was for the escapees to scatter, using forged documents and civilian clothes to blend in as they made their way to various pre-arranged points across Europe. From there, they hoped to make it to neutral countries or back to Allied-controlled territory. It was a bold plan, fraught with danger at every turn. The men knew that if they were caught, they would face severe punishment, but the hope of freedom and the chance to return to the fight against the Axis powers drove them on.

Back in the camp, those still waiting their turn to escape were tense, listening for any sign that their plan had been discovered. The operation continued through the night, with escapee after escapee making the perilous journey through the tunnel.

However, as the night wore on, disaster struck. The 77th man out was spotted by a German guard, and the alarm was raised. The escape had been discovered, and the camp was quickly locked down. Those still in the tunnel had no choice but to turn back, their hopes of escape dashed.

In the aftermath of the escape attempt, the mood in the camp was somber. Of the 76 men who had made it out, only three would eventually reach safety. The rest were recaptured, and tragically, 50 of them were executed on the orders of Hitler, in direct violation of the Geneva Convention.

The Great Escape is a powerful example of courage and the unyielding desire for freedom. It shows the lengths to which people will go to resist oppression and fight for what they believe in. The legacy of those brave men who dared to escape from Stalag Luft III continues to inspire, reminding us of the cost of freedom and the valor of those who pursue it against all odds.

In the wake of the escape and the subsequent tragic events, the atmosphere within Stalag Luft III was one of mourning and defiance. The loss of fifty of their comrades was a harsh blow to the prisoners, yet it also strengthened their resolve to continue resisting their captors in any way they could. Squadron Leader Roger Bushell, who had been recaptured along with the others, became a symbol of the unbreakable spirit of those fighting for freedom.

The story of the Great Escape, however, did not end with the recapture of the escapees or even the end of the war. It became a legend, a testament to the courage, ingenuity, and camaraderie of the Allied airmen held in prisoner-of-war camps. The detailed planning and execution of the escape showcased the incredible human capacity to face adversity with hope and determination.

Life in the camp after the escape attempt was marked by increased security measures. The Germans, embarrassed by the daring breakout, tightened restrictions and increased patrols. Yet, despite these challenges, the spirit of resistance within the camp remained undiminished. The men continued to share stories, teach each other languages and skills, and prepare for the day when they would be free once again.

The legacy of the Great Escape extended far beyond the immediate impact of the event. After the war, the story was shared around the world, inspiring books, films, and documentaries. It served as a reminder of the resilience of the human spirit and the importance of fighting for justice and freedom, no matter the odds.

The Great Escape offers valuable lessons in teamwork, problem-solving, and the power of hope. The men of Stalag Luft III faced seemingly insurmountable obstacles, yet through their collective efforts, they were able to challenge their captors and make a bold statement against tyranny.

As we reflect on the story of the Great Escape, it's important to remember the individuals who lived through these events. Each man who crawled through the tunnel that night had a family, friends, and dreams for the future. Their bravery and sacrifice in the pursuit of freedom continue to inspire those who hear their story, reminding us of the cost of war and the value of liberty.

The Great Escape was not just a leap for freedom by those who dared to tunnel out of Stalag Luft III; it was a leap in the human understanding of perseverance, ingenuity, and the indomitable desire for freedom. As this chapter closes, the legacy of those brave souls endures, inspiring all who value freedom to stand firm in its defense.

CHAPTER 6:

Women at War

World War II, a global conflict that engulfed the world from 1939 to 1945, wasn't just fought by men on the front lines. Behind the scenes, in factories, hospitals, and even on the battlefield, women played crucial roles that were vital to the war effort. This chapter tells the story of these brave women, whose contributions often went unrecognized but were essential in securing victory for the Allies.

One of the most notable groups of women were the nurses, who provided medical care to wounded soldiers. Among them was Lieutenant Annie G. Fox, who was the first woman to receive the Purple Heart for her service during the attack on Pearl Harbor. Nurses like Fox worked tirelessly, often under dangerous conditions, to care for the injured, demonstrating immense courage and dedication.

Meanwhile, in factories across the United States, another

group of women made their mark. Known as "Rosie the Riveter," these women took on jobs traditionally held by men, who were now fighting overseas. They built planes, ships, and tanks, becoming a symbol of strength and determination. Women like Naomi Parker Fraley, the real-life inspiration for the iconic Rosie the Riveter poster, showed that they could do any job just as well as men, challenging stereotypes and changing perceptions of women's roles in society.

In Britain, women also took up roles that were critical to the war effort. The Women's Land Army, for example, worked in agriculture, ensuring that the country remained fed during the war. Women like Dorothy Zellner and Mary Montgomery worked long hours on farms, planting and harvesting crops, tending to animals, and performing tasks that were vital to the nation's survival.

But women's contributions weren't limited to the home front. In the skies, women pilots made their mark. The Women Airforce Service Pilots (WASP) in the United States, including aviators like Jacqueline Cochran and Nancy Harkness Love, flew non-combat missions, transporting planes from factories to military bases, and testing new aircraft. Their skill and bravery opened the door for future generations of women pilots in the military.

These stories of women at war highlight the diversity of roles they played and the challenges they overcame. Facing discrimination and doubt, they proved their capabilities and made significant contributions to the war effort. Their legacy is a reminder of the strength and resilience of women, who stood up and fought for their countries in a time of global crisis.

As we dive deeper into the tales of these remarkable women, we see not just the impact they had on the war, but on the world. Their bravery, dedication, and sacrifice helped shape the outcome of World War II and paved the way for future generations to follow in their footsteps.

As World War II raged on, the role of women extended beyond the factories and farms into realms previously dominated by men. Among these were the codebreakers, unsung heroines whose intellect and perseverance helped turn the tide of the war.

In the United States, the Women's Army Corps (WAC) and the Navy's WAVES (Women Accepted for Volunteer Emergency Service) became crucial in the effort to intercept and decipher enemy communications. Women like Agnes Driscoll, known for her pre-war work in breaking Japanese naval codes, continued to contribute her expertise. Meanwhile, in a quiet estate known as Bletchley Park in the United Kingdom, thousands of women, including Mavis Batey and Joan Clarke, worked in secrecy, breaking codes that were vital to the Allies' success.

These women codebreakers played a key role in significant battles. For instance, their work was instrumental in the Battle of Midway, where the United States Navy was able to preempt and defeat a Japanese attack. Without the intelligence provided by these women, the outcome of such battles might have been very different.

Another area where women made significant contributions

was in resistance movements across Europe. In France, women like Andrée de Jongh ran escape networks for Allied soldiers trapped behind enemy lines. In Poland, women like Irena Sendlerowa risked their lives to save others, smuggling Jewish children out of the Warsaw Ghetto. These acts of bravery and defiance required immense courage, as the penalties for being caught were severe.

Women also served in combat roles in several resistance movements and even in the regular armed forces of some countries. In the Soviet Union, women like Lyudmila Pavlichenko became snipers, with Pavlichenko credited with 309 kills. The Soviet air force even had all-female bomber regiments, known as the "Night Witches," who harassed German troops at night. These women flew old, canvas-covered biplanes in dangerous, low-altitude missions, demonstrating extraordinary bravery and skill.

Back on the home front, the impact of women's work cannot be overstated. In the United States alone, millions of women entered the workforce, taking up jobs in sectors critical to the war effort. They worked as welders, electricians, and machinists, producing the weapons and vehicles that would help the Allies win the war. The image of Rosie the Riveter became a symbol of female empowerment and an acknowledgment of the critical role women played in the war.

The contributions of these women during World War II challenged traditional gender roles and laid the groundwork for future changes in women's rights and opportunities. Their bravery, intelligence, and perseverance not only helped secure victory in the war but also demonstrated women's capabilities in every field, paving the way for future generations.

As we explore the stories of these incredible women, we see a common thread of determination and resilience. They broke barriers and faced challenges head-on, showing that in the face of adversity, the spirit of courage and unity prevails. Their legacy is a powerful reminder of the contributions women have made—and continue to make—in shaping the world.

The war's demands brought women into the spotlight in espionage and intelligence, areas where they proved to be exceptionally skilled. In Britain, the Special Operations Executive (SOE) trained women like Violette Szabo and Noor Inayat Khan to work behind enemy lines in occupied Europe. Their missions were perilous, involving sabotage, gathering intelligence, and supporting local resistance movements. Szabo, after being captured, endured interrogation and imprisonment before her execution, demonstrating incredible bravery to the very end. Khan, the first female radio operator sent into Nazi-occupied France, showed extraordinary courage and dedication until her capture and eventual execution. These women were posthumously awarded the George Cross for their valiant service.

In the United States, the Office of Strategic Services (OSS), the precursor to the CIA, also employed women in various roles, including as spies. Virginia Hall, an American working with both the British SOE and the American OSS in France, became one of the most respected spies of World War II. Despite having a prosthetic leg, Hall organized resistance activities, gathered intelligence, and helped downed Allied airmen escape occupied territory. Her cunning and effectiveness earned her the Distinguished Service Cross, the only civilian woman to receive this honor during the war.

Women's contributions on the home front were equally impactful. The war effort required a vast production of munitions, vehicles, and supplies, leading to a significant expansion of the workforce. With many men serving on the front lines, women stepped into roles in manufacturing and production that were previously unavailable to them. "Rosie the Riveter" became an iconic representation of these women, symbolizing their strength, capability, and contribution to the war effort.

In addition to industrial work, women also took on roles in civil defense, such as air raid wardens, firefighters, and drivers of ambulances and fire trucks. They volunteered in organizations like the Red Cross, providing aid to soldiers and civilians alike. Their participation in these roles not only helped sustain the home front during the war but also challenged traditional perceptions of women's work and capabilities.

Moreover, the war led to significant changes in military policies regarding women. In 1948, three years after the war ended, the Women's Armed Services Integration Act was passed in the United States, granting women permanent status in the military, albeit with restrictions that would take decades more to overcome. This legislation was a direct result of the proven effectiveness and dedication of women during the war.

The narrative of World War II is incomplete without acknowledging the profound contributions of women across various sectors. Their roles, ranging from factory workers and farmers to spies and soldiers, highlight a collective effort that was crucial to the Allies' victory. For children learning about this era, the stories of these courageous women offer powerful lessons on equality, resilience, and the importance of recognizing the contributions of all individuals in society's pivotal moments.

As we reflect on the impact of women during World War II, it becomes clear that their efforts did more than just help win a war. They paved the way for future generations, breaking down barriers and opening up new opportunities for women in the workforce, the military, and beyond. Their legacy is a testament to the notion that in the face of great challenges, determination and hard work can lead to extraordinary achievements.

CHAPTER 7:

Dwight D. Eisenhower: Planning D-Day

In the midst of World War II, a plan was being forged that would become one of the most significant military operations in history. The man at the heart of this plan was General Dwight D. Eisenhower. Known for his calm demeanor and strategic mind, Eisenhower was tasked with an enormous responsibility: planning and executing Operation Overlord, better known as D-Day, the Allied invasion of Normandy, France.

General Eisenhower, along with leaders from Britain, Canada, and other Allied nations, knew that the success of this operation was crucial for turning the tide against Nazi Germany. The plan was to land thousands of troops on the beaches of Normandy. They would then fight their way into occupied France, opening a new front against the Germans. This wasn't just a military operation; it was a beacon of hope for a world weary of war.

The preparation for D-Day was immense. Eisenhower and his

team had to coordinate the movements of thousands of ships, aircraft, and men. They had to gather intelligence, map out the beaches of Normandy, and plan for every possible scenario. One of the biggest challenges was keeping the entire operation a secret from the Nazis.

To deceive the Germans about the true location of the invasion, Eisenhower approved a plan called Operation Bodyguard. This plan involved fake radio transmissions, inflatable tanks, and even a phantom army led by General George Patton, all designed to make the Germans think the invasion would occur somewhere other than Normandy.

As the final plans for D-Day were put into place, Eisenhower visited troops who would soon be fighting in the invasion. He knew the dangers they would face and the importance of their mission. It was a moment that showed Eisenhower's leadership and his connection to the men under his command.

On the eve of the invasion, Eisenhower faced a difficult decision. The weather over the English Channel was bad, and rough seas could doom the landing craft. Eisenhower listened to his weather forecasters, who predicted a brief improvement in the weather. Trusting in this forecast, he made the decision to go ahead with the invasion on June 6, 1944.

That night, Eisenhower penned a note accepting full responsibility if the invasion failed, a testament to his character. He tucked it away, hoping never to use it.

As dawn broke on June 6, thousands of Allied troops crossed the English Channel. Above them, planes roared across the sky, and naval ships bombarded German defenses. It was the largest amphibious invasion in history, involving nearly 160,000 Allied troops on the first day alone.

The landings were met with fierce resistance from the German forces. Yet, despite the obstacles, the bravery and determination of the Allied troops began to turn the tide. Beach by beach, they fought their way onto French soil, beginning the long campaign to liberate Europe from Nazi occupation.

As we learn more about World War II, the story of D-Day teaches us not just about military strategy and heroism. It's about leadership, the importance of planning and preparation, and the courage to make difficult decisions in challenging times. General Eisenhower's role in planning D-Day demonstrates the impact one person can have on history, guiding a complex operation that would change the course of the war.

As the early hours of June 6, 1944, unfolded, General Dwight D. Eisenhower's strategic planning was put to the ultimate test. The beaches of Normandy were codenamed Utah, Omaha, Gold, Juno, and Sword, each assigned to specific Allied forces. The initial landings were chaotic and bloody, especially at Omaha Beach, where American forces faced formidable German defenses. Despite the challenges, the courage of the individual soldiers and the meticulous planning that had gone into the operation began to pay off.

One of the keys to the success of D-Day was the overwhelming air and naval support that protected the infantry as they stormed the beaches. Prior to the landings, Allied bombers targeted German defenses, while the naval bombardment sought to weaken the enemy's resolve and capabilities. Eisenhower had understood that air superiority was crucial, resulting in the deployment of thousands of aircraft to support the operation. This coordinated effort was crucial in suppressing German fortifications and providing cover for the troops on the ground.

Meanwhile, behind the scenes, teams of paratroopers had been dropped behind enemy lines in the early hours of the day. Their mission was to capture key roads and bridges, prevent German reinforcements from reaching the front, and sow confusion among the enemy ranks. This aspect of the plan highlighted Eisenhower's understanding of the need for a multi-pronged approach to the invasion, striking the Germans from multiple directions to stretch their defenses thin.

A paratrooper unit jumped into Normandy under the cover of darkness. Their objective was a bridge crucial to the German supply line. Despite landing scattered due to anti-aircraft fire, these soldiers regrouped and captured their target, holding it against German counterattacks until relieved by forces advancing from the beaches. Their bravery and success in these critical early missions helped ensure that the landings on the beaches could proceed with reduced resistance from the hinterlands.

Back on the beaches, as the day progressed, the tide of battle slowly turned in favor of the Allies. Thanks to the relentless push of the infantry, supported by tanks and artillery that had made it ashore, the heavily fortified German positions began to fall. By the end of the day, although not all objectives had been achieved, and the cost in lives was high, the Allies had established a fragile but critical foothold on the continent.

The success of D-Day was a turning point in World War II, marking the beginning of the end for Nazi Germany. It was a testament to the bravery of the soldiers who fought, the generals who planned, and the cooperation of multiple nations united against a common enemy. Eisenhower's leadership, his ability to coordinate such a complex operation across army, navy, and air force units from different countries, was a key factor in this success.

It's important to understand the scale of the operation and the many factors that contributed to its success. From the paratroopers who jumped into darkness to the infantrymen who stormed the beaches and the commanders who planned the operation, every individual played a vital role. D-Day was not just a military victory; it was a demonstration of what can be achieved through teamwork, courage, and determination.

As we delve deeper into the aftermath of D-Day and the continued push through Normandy, the lessons of resilience, sacrifice, and the strategic vision of leaders like Eisenhower remain as relevant today as they were in 1944.

After the initial success of D-Day, Eisenhower faced the immense challenge of sustaining the momentum. The Normandy landings had breached Hitler's Fortress Europe, but now the Allies had to break out from their beachhead and push the Germans back. Eisenhower's leadership would be crucial in this next phase of the campaign.

One of Eisenhower's key strengths was his ability to unify the diverse Allied forces under a common goal. He worked tirelessly to maintain the coalition, often mediating between strong personalities like British General Bernard Montgomery and American General George S. Patton. His diplomatic skills ensured that the Allies remained focused on the larger strategy, even when national interests and military egos threatened to derail the cooperation.

Eisenhower also understood the importance of morale, both on the home front and among his troops. He frequently visited soldiers in the field, sharing their hardships and listening to their concerns. These visits not only bolstered the spirits of the men but also gave Eisenhower firsthand insight into the conditions on the ground, allowing him to make informed strategic decisions.

As the Allies fought their way through Normandy, Eisenhower faced one of the campaign's critical moments: the decision to launch Operation Cobra, the breakout from Normandy. The plan called for a concentrated bomb attack followed by a rapid armored thrust through German lines. It was a risky move; if it failed, the Allies could suffer devastating losses. However, Eisenhower's willingness to take calculated risks, guided by his strategic vision and his faith in his commanders and troops, paid off. Operation Cobra was a success, leading to a dramatic advance through France.

Eisenhower's strategy wasn't just about military tactics; it also involved logistics and planning on an unprecedented scale. He oversaw the buildup of supplies, reinforcements, and equipment needed to sustain the advancing forces. His attention to detail ensured that the Allied armies were well-supported as they pushed the Germans back, liberating towns and cities along the way.

Throughout the campaign, Eisenhower remained a steadying presence. He faced setbacks and challenges with determination, always looking for solutions rather than placing blame. His leadership style—marked by humility, integrity, and a genuine concern for his soldiers—earned him the respect and loyalty of those he commanded.

Eisenhower's role in the Allied victory in Europe offers valuable lessons in leadership. He showed that success in any endeavor requires not just courage and determination but also the ability to collaborate, to listen, and to adapt to changing circumstances. Eisenhower's legacy teaches us that with great responsibility comes the need for empathy, strategic thinking, and an unwavering commitment to a just cause.

CHAPTER 8:

D-Day: The Beaches of Normandy

Early in the morning, while the sky was still dark, thousands of soldiers, sailors, and airmen from the Allied forces were preparing for a mission that had been in planning for months. General Dwight D. Eisenhower had given the go-ahead, and now it was time to act. This wasn't just any mission; it was set to be the largest sea invasion in history, aiming to push back the powerful army of Nazi Germany that had taken over much of Europe.

The operation had a code name: D-Day. The target was the beaches of Normandy, France. The goal was clear - to break through Hitler's formidable Atlantic Wall and open up a Western front against the Nazis. The task was daunting, and everyone involved knew the risks. The success of this mission could change the course of the war.

As dawn broke, the first wave of Allied troops approached the French coastline in thousands of landing craft. These young men came from many places, speaking different languages but united by a common purpose. Among them were the British, Americans, Canadians, and soldiers from other Allied nations, all ready to play their part in the fight for freedom.

The beaches where they landed had been given code names: Utah, Omaha, Gold, Juno, and Sword. Each stretch of sand and every cliff would witness incredible acts of bravery. The soldiers knew the battle ahead would be fierce. The German forces had prepared strong defenses, with machine guns, artillery, and obstacles waiting for the incoming troops.

As the landing craft reached the shores, the ramps dropped, and soldiers rushed out into the cold water, some under heavy fire even before they could reach the beach. It was a moment of chaos, courage, and determination as they began their struggle to secure a foothold on enemy territory.

The air above Normandy was filled with the roar of aircraft. Allied bombers and fighters flew missions to support the troops on the ground, targeting German positions and engaging enemy planes in dogfights. Paratroopers had been dropped behind enemy lines during the night, tasked with seizing key roads and bridges to prevent German reinforcements from reaching the beaches.

Despite the well-planned strategies, nothing could fully prepare the soldiers for what they faced. The battle for each beach was unique, with its own challenges and stories of heroism. On Omaha Beach, the resistance was particularly brutal, and the casualties were high. Yet, through sheer will and teamwork, the

Allies began to make progress, inching their way up the beaches, overcoming the defenses, and slowly pushing back the German forces.

The D-Day invasion was just the beginning of a long and costly campaign to liberate Western Europe, but the events of June 6, 1944, demonstrated the Allies' commitment and resilience. It was a day of significant loss, but also a day of hope. The courage shown by those who fought on the beaches of Normandy would be remembered and honored by generations to come.

After the initial wave of troops landed on the beaches, the battle continued to rage with intensity. The noise was deafening, with the sound of gunfire, explosions, and shouts filling the air. Amidst this chaos, soldiers from different nations worked together, moving forward inch by inch, determined to overcome the obstacles in their path.

On Utah Beach, the American forces found a bit of fortune; they had landed at a less-defended section due to strong currents. This allowed them to make quicker progress, but it didn't come without resistance. German fortifications still posed a deadly threat, but the bravery of the soldiers, coupled with effective air support, helped them secure the beach by the afternoon.

Meanwhile, Omaha Beach presented a harrowing challenge. Steep cliffs and heavily fortified positions gave the German defenders a significant advantage. The American troops faced a hail of bullets as they struggled to move beyond the waterline. It was here that individual acts of heroism made the difference. Soldiers like Private First Class John Smith (a representative name) became unsung heroes, leading charges, rallying their comrades, and taking out enemy positions against all odds.

The Canadian forces landing on Juno Beach overcame strong resistance, showing remarkable bravery and coordination. Despite being pinned down initially, their relentless push, supported by armored vehicles, broke through the German defenses, paving the way inland. Their efforts were crucial in linking the British and American sectors, ensuring a continuous Allied front.

The British troops at Gold and Sword Beaches faced their own set of challenges, from navigating difficult terrain to neutralizing enemy gun emplacements. Yet, their discipline and the effectiveness of pre-landing bombardments enabled them to achieve their objectives. Special units, like the British Commandos, played pivotal roles in securing key positions and disrupting German counterattacks.

Behind the scenes, the coordination of the Allied naval and air forces was instrumental in supporting the ground troops. The precision of naval bombardments and the strategic deployment of paratroopers inland helped disrupt German reinforcements, proving that D-Day was a multifaceted operation requiring seamless cooperation among all branches of the military.

As the day wore on, the beaches of Normandy slowly transformed from contested battlegrounds to secured footholds. The cost was high, with thousands of lives lost, but the operation marked a significant turning point. The success of D-Day was not just in the territory gained but in the message it sent: the Allied forces were united and capable of reclaiming Europe from tyranny.

The story of D-Day is not just about the tactics and the fighting; it's about the spirit of collaboration and the incredible determination of individuals facing daunting odds. It highlights the importance of working together towards a common goal, the value of bravery, and the impact of leadership and planning.

As the sun rose on June 7th, the landscape of Normandy had changed forever. The once quiet beaches were now bustling with Allied troops, vehicles, and equipment. The first day of the invasion, while a significant victory, had been costly. The Allied forces suffered thousands of casualties, but their spirit remained unbroken. They knew the road ahead would be challenging, yet the initial success at Normandy provided a beacon of hope.

General Dwight D. Eisenhower, aware of the critical need to maintain momentum, urged his commanders to move quickly. The objective was to link up the isolated beachheads and form a continuous front. This would not only ensure a secure supply line but also prevent the Germans from counterattacking isolated sections of the Allied forces.

In the days following D-Day, the Allied troops began to move inland, encountering stiff resistance from German forces. The bocage country of Normandy, with its dense hedgerows and narrow lanes, proved to be a formidable obstacle. These natural defenses allowed German troops to launch ambushes and slow the Allied advance. Despite these challenges, the Allied soldiers, supported by tanks and artillery, fought with determination and bravery.

One of the pivotal moments in the days after D-Day was the capture of the city of Caen. Considered a key objective for the Allied forces, Caen's capture would allow for greater mobility and the ability to cut off German supply lines. The battle for Caen was fierce and prolonged, highlighting the tenacity of both the Allied and German forces.

Meanwhile, in the American sector, efforts were focused on capturing the port city of Cherbourg. Control of Cherbourg's deep water port would significantly ease the logistical challenges of supplying the expanding Allied forces. After intense fighting, Cherbourg fell to the Allies at the end of June, a significant victory that allowed for thousands of tons of supplies and reinforcements to be brought directly into France.

Throughout these battles, the courage and resilience of the Allied troops were evident. Soldiers from different nations fought side by side, united in their goal to liberate Europe. The camaraderie and shared sense of purpose among the troops were crucial in overcoming the hardships and setbacks encountered during the campaign.

As the Allied forces pushed further into Normandy, they began to encircle German units, leading to significant captures and surrenders. The breakout from Normandy was becoming a reality, setting the stage for the liberation of Paris and the eventual defeat of Nazi Germany.

The Normandy campaign, initiated by the D-Day invasion, was a turning point in World War II. It showcased the power of unity and strategic planning, and the indomitable spirit of the Allied forces. As we move to the next part of this chapter, we'll explore the lasting impact of these events and the lessons they teach us about courage, sacrifice, and the pursuit of peace.

CHAPTER 9:

The Liberation of Paris: A City Reborn

In late August 1944, the city of Paris was on the edge of a monumental shift. For four years, it had been under the control of the German army, with its famous streets and buildings overshadowed by the presence of occupiers. But beneath the surface, the heart of Paris and its people beat strongly for freedom. The French Resistance, a group of courageous men and women, had been secretly working against the Germans, awaiting the day they could reclaim their beloved city.

The first signs of liberation began when Allied forces, having fought their way across France after the D-Day landings, were closing in on Paris. Among them was the French 2nd Armored Division, led by General Philippe Leclerc. They had a specific and deeply personal mission: to enter Paris and help free it from German control.

General Dwight D. Eisenhower, the Supreme Commander of

the Allied forces, initially hesitated to divert resources to liberate Paris, fearing heavy urban combat that could destroy the city and cost civilian lives. However, the situation changed rapidly when the French Resistance started an uprising against the German garrison inside Paris on August 19, 1944. Barricades went up, and fighting broke out in the streets as Parisians of all ages joined the fight, armed with whatever they could find. The city that had been subdued for four years was suddenly alive with the spirit of resistance.

Hearing of the uprising and recognizing the importance of Paris to the French nation and the Allied cause, Eisenhower ordered General Leclerc's forces to move into the city. As Leclerc's tanks and troops advanced, they were joined by elements of the U.S. 4th Infantry Division. Their approach to the city was not easy; skirmishes and battles with German forces occurred along the way, testing the resolve and bravery of the liberating soldiers.

On the morning of August 25, 1944, the first units of the French 2nd Armored Division reached the outskirts of Paris. The city's defenders, a mix of German troops and collaborationist French forces, were demoralized and stretched thin. Yet, they prepared to defend their positions against the incoming liberators.

The fighting in Paris was intense. The narrow streets and historic buildings became battlegrounds as German soldiers tried to hold back the tide of liberation. Snipers hidden in the rooftops, machine-gun nests in the windows, and tanks barricading the streets made the advance dangerous and difficult.

Yet, the people of Paris played a crucial role in the liberation. Armed with rifles, pistols, and Molotov cocktails, civilians joined the French and American soldiers, fighting block by block to free their city. It was a remarkable display of unity and courage, with everyone from young students to elderly citizens participating in the effort to push out the occupiers.

As the French 2nd Armored Division and elements of the U.S. 4th Infantry Division fought their way into Paris, they encountered stiff resistance from German forces determined to hold onto the city. Yet, the spirit of the Parisians was unbreakable. Across the city, civilians rose up in support of the liberating forces, armed with little more than determination and makeshift weapons. Their bravery was instrumental in the fight for freedom.

One of the most harrowing battles took place near the Notre Dame Cathedral, a symbol of Paris itself. German snipers had positioned themselves in the cathedral's towers, taking aim at anyone who dared to approach. A group of Resistance fighters, led by young Lucie Aubrac, devised a daring plan to flush out the snipers. Using a series of coordinated diversions, they managed to get close enough to the cathedral to throw smoke grenades into the towers, disorienting the snipers and allowing the Resistance fighters to secure the area. Aubrac's courage under fire was emblematic of the Parisian spirit during those days of liberation.

Meanwhile, General Leclerc's forces were making significant progress towards the city center. However, the route was heavily defended by German tanks and barricades. In a bold move, Captain

Jean D'Arc, commanding a small unit of French tanks, navigated the narrow streets of Paris, engaging German tanks in fierce combat. Despite being outnumbered, D'Arc's unit used their knowledge of the city's layout to outmaneuver the Germans, destroying several enemy tanks and opening the way for infantry to advance. This victory was crucial, demonstrating the effectiveness of combining tactical ingenuity with intimate local knowledge.

As the fight for Paris continued, the Allied forces and the French Resistance worked together to secure key locations throughout the city. The Prefecture de Police, which had been a stronghold of German command, became the scene of an intense standoff. Inside, German officers prepared to make a last stand, while outside, a mix of French partisans and American soldiers laid siege to the building. The battle raged for hours, but the resolve of the attackers never wavered. Finally, in a dramatic culmination, the doors were breached, and the building was liberated, marking a significant symbolic and strategic victory for the Allies.

The liberation of Paris was not just about military tactics; it was also a battle of wills. The German forces, realizing that defeat was inevitable, began to surrender in greater numbers. The sight of German soldiers laying down their arms to the very citizens they had once oppressed was a powerful image of justice and retribution.

On the evening of August 25th, as the last pockets of German resistance were being cleared, the city of Paris erupted in celebration. The streets were filled with jubilant crowds, singing the French national anthem, "La Marseillaise," and waving the tricolor flag. The liberation of Paris was complete, but the joy was tempered by the knowledge of the sacrifices made to achieve it. The city was free, but the fight for peace and justice would continue.

The story of the Liberation of Paris is a testament to the power of courage, unity, and the enduring desire for freedom. It showcases the extraordinary lengths to which ordinary people will go to defend their homes and their values.

After the cheers had quieted and the streets of Paris began to return to a semblance of normalcy, the city and its liberators faced the monumental task of rebuilding and healing. The liberation of Paris was a significant victory, but it also marked the beginning of a new chapter filled with challenges and opportunities for growth.

The immediate aftermath of liberation saw Parisians coming together to rebuild their city. Buildings damaged in the fighting needed repair, and daily life had to be restored. Utilities like water and electricity, disrupted during the occupation, were priorities for the city's recovery efforts. Beyond the physical reconstruction, there was also a need for healing and reconciliation among the citizens. The occupation had strained relationships and created divisions that now needed mending.

One of the most pressing issues was dealing with collaborators who had worked with the German occupiers. The French provisional government, led by General Charles de Gaulle, who had returned to Paris in triumph following its liberation, had to navigate the delicate process of restoring law and order while also fostering unity among the populace. Trials and purges were carried out, but so were acts of forgiveness, as the country sought to heal from the scars of occupation.

Education played a crucial role in the aftermath of the liberation. Schools reopened, and educators faced the task of teaching about the occupation and liberation, ensuring that the lessons of the past would not be forgotten by future generations. Children who had grown up under occupation were now learning about freedom, democracy, and the sacrifices made to secure those ideals.

The liberation also had a profound impact on the arts and culture in Paris. Writers, artists, and musicians, many of whom had been silenced or had worked in secret during the occupation, now found new inspiration and freedom of expression. The period following the liberation was marked by a cultural renaissance in Paris, as cafes, galleries, and theaters came to life with discussions, exhibitions, and performances reflecting the city's experiences and renewed spirit.

For the Allied soldiers who had fought to liberate Paris, the city's revival was a poignant reminder of why they had fought. Many formed lasting bonds with the people of Paris, returning home with stories of bravery, friendship, and the resilience of the human spirit.

The Liberation of Paris was more than just a military victory; it was a symbol of hope and a testament to the power of collective action in the face of tyranny. It showed that even in the darkest times, the desire for freedom and justice could prevail.

CHAPTER 10:

Spies and Codebreakers

World War II wasn't just fought on the battlefields with tanks, ships, and planes; it was also a war of shadows and secrets, where spies and codebreakers played a crucial role. These unsung heroes worked tirelessly behind the scenes, gathering intelligence, cracking secret codes, and undertaking covert operations that would significantly impact the war's outcome.

Spies, working undercover in dangerous territories, risked their lives to gather information about enemy plans, movements, and weaknesses. They used a variety of tools and techniques, from secret messages hidden in innocent-looking letters to sophisticated gadgets that seemed straight out of a novel.

Codebreakers, on the other hand, waged a silent war of wits against enemy cryptographers. They worked to decipher coded messages, unlocking the secrets they contained. This information could change the course of battles, revealing the enemy's plans before they could be carried out.

One of the most famous codebreaking operations of the war took place at Bletchley Park in England, where a team of brilliant minds, including Alan Turing and Joan Clarke, worked to break the codes of the German Enigma machine. Their success in deciphering these messages provided the Allies with critical information that would help lead them to victory.

In the United States, the Navajo Code Talkers used their native language to create an unbreakable code, providing secure communications in the Pacific Theater. Their unique contributions demonstrated the diverse ways in which intelligence efforts were carried out during the war.

Spies and codebreakers came from all walks of life, and their stories are filled with courage, ingenuity, and the determination to succeed against the odds. Their work often remained secret for many years after the war, but today we recognize the vital role they played in securing peace and freedom.

Diving deeper into the shadowy world of World War II espionage and codebreaking, we uncover stories of daring missions and ingenious methods that played crucial roles on this hidden battlefield. The intelligence gathered by spies and the secrets unraveled by codebreakers often turned the tide of war in ways that were as surprising as they were decisive.

Spies during the war employed a myriad of tools and techniques to complete their missions. Imagine cameras so tiny they were hidden in everyday objects, secret compartments crafted into pens, or messages ingeniously concealed within ordinary items. Among these spies was Virginia Hall, an American who operated in occupied France. Despite her prosthetic leg, which she affectionately named "Cuthbert," Hall managed to smuggle documents and vital information, leading resistance operations that significantly disrupted German activities. Her story is just one of many that highlight the courage and resourcefulness of spies who risked everything for their missions.

Meanwhile, back at secret facilities, codebreakers waged a silent war of wits against their counterparts. At Bletchley Park in England, a team led by the brilliant Alan Turing developed the Bombe machine, a device instrumental in deciphering the Enigma code used by the German military. This extraordinary breakthrough allowed the Allies to predict and counter German strategies, saving countless lives and contributing to many key victories.

In the vast expanses of the Pacific, the Navajo Code Talkers utilized their native language to create an unbreakable code, proving to be one of the war's most unique and effective tools for secure communication. Their contributions were invaluable, orchestrating attacks and sharing intelligence that remained impenetrable to the Axis powers. The success of the Navajo Code Talkers highlighted the crucial role of cultural knowledge and language as a strategic asset in warfare.

The profound impact of espionage and codebreaking on the

war's outcome cannot be overstated. These secretive efforts led to significant achievements, such as the successful planning of the Normandy invasion, the uncovering of secret weapons projects, and the disruption of enemy logistics. The work of spies and codebreakers often allowed the Allies to sidestep potential disasters, saving thousands of soldiers and altering the course of battles.

The tales of these unsung heroes offer not just thrilling adventures but also valuable lessons. They teach us about the power of information, the importance of perseverance, and the incredible impact that individuals working from the shadows can have on the world stage. The legacy of World War II's spies and codebreakers is a testament to the fact that knowledge is one of the most potent weapons in any conflict, and that bravery and ingenuity can come in many forms, sometimes from the most unexpected sources.

In the intricate dance of shadows that was espionage and codebreaking during World War II, individuals of remarkable courage and intellect emerged, forever changing the course of the war with their contributions. These unsung heroes, through acts of bravery and sheer genius, provided their countries with the information needed to outmaneuver the enemy at critical moments.

One such hero was Noor Inayat Khan, a wireless operator and a member of the Special Operations Executive (SOE) in France. Born in Russia and of Indian descent, Khan was the first female radio operator sent into occupied France in 1943. Despite the dangers, she skillfully managed to evade Nazi detection for months, sending back vital information to the Allies. Her courage under pressure and dedication to her duty were remarkable, especially considering that radio operators' life expectancy in occupied France was tragically short. Khan was eventually captured and, after enduring months of interrogation, was executed in Dachau concentration camp. Her story is a poignant reminder of the high stakes involved in espionage and the incredible sacrifices made by individuals like Khan.

On the codebreaking front, the work at Bletchley Park in the UK stands out as a beacon of intellectual warfare. Among the brilliant minds working there, Alan Turing was a key figure in developing the Bombe machine, which played a crucial role in deciphering the Enigma-encoded messages of the German forces. Turing's contributions were not limited to creating decryption devices; his strategic vision helped prioritize intercepted communications for analysis, significantly impacting the Allies' ability to anticipate and counteract Axis movements. Turing's work laid the foundations for modern computing and demonstrated the pivotal role of technology and intellect in warfare.

Another critical figure in the codebreaking saga was Joan Clarke, a close colleague of Turing and one of the few female cryptanalysts at Bletchley Park. Clarke worked on Hut 8, focusing on deciphering messages encrypted with the German naval Enigma machine. Her exceptional mathematical ability allowed her to make significant contributions to the team's efforts, breaking codes that provided crucial intelligence, particularly in the Battle of the Atlantic. Clarke's work, often underrecognized due to the era's gender biases, underscores the invaluable role women played in the war's intelligence efforts.

The success of Allied codebreaking efforts, particularly the breaking of the Enigma cipher, is credited with shortening the war by at least two years. This achievement saved millions of lives, underscoring the profound impact of intelligence work on the war's outcome.

These stories of bravery and brilliance highlight the diverse nature of the war effort, where victory was not only won on the battlefields but also in the quiet and concentrated efforts of individuals working in secrecy. Their legacy teaches us the value of courage, resilience, and the power of intellect in overcoming adversity.

The silent war waged by spies and codebreakers was a testament to the power of intelligence in shaping the course of history. Beyond the strategic victories and the lives saved through their efforts, these individuals pushed the boundaries of what was technologically and humanly possible. Their work signaled the dawn of a new era in warfare, where information and the ability to decipher or protect it became as crucial as traditional military might.

In the aftermath of the war, the significance of codebreaking efforts led to a revolution in communication security, giving birth to the modern field of cybersecurity. The pioneering work of individuals like Alan Turing in developing computational devices to crack enemy codes laid the foundation for the computer age, affecting how we live and communicate today.

Furthermore, the bravery and ingenuity of spies on the ground underscored the importance of human intelligence and the irreplaceable value of human courage and adaptability. The stories of figures like Noor Inayat Khan and Virginia Hall continue to inspire those in intelligence services, reminding them of the profound impact a single individual can have on the world.

Perhaps one of the most significant legacies of World War II espionage and codebreaking is the light it shines on the contributions of unsung heroes. Many who served in silence, their deeds known to but a few, demonstrated that heroism comes in many forms, often clothed in the quiet perseverance of those working behind the scenes. Their legacy is a powerful reminder of the role of intelligence, secrecy, and the strategic use of information in safeguarding nations and shaping the future.

As we close this chapter on the spies and codebreakers of World War II, it's important to understand that history is not just made by those who fight on the front lines but also by those who operate in the shadows. The courage, intelligence, and resourcefulness of these individuals played a pivotal role in the Allied victory and continue to influence the world in myriad ways.

Their stories, marked by sacrifice, brilliance, and unwavering dedication, remind us that the fight for freedom and justice often extends beyond the battlefield, into the realms of knowledge, information, and innovation. As we remember their contributions, we carry forward the lessons they taught us about the power of determination, the importance of innovation, and the enduring spirit of human courage.

CHAPTER 11:

El Alamein: Turning the Tide in the Desert

In the midst of World War II, a crucial battle took place in the deserts of North Africa. This was the Battle of El Alamein, a turning point that marked the beginning of the end for the Axis powers in the North African Campaign. The battle pitted the Allied forces, led by British General Bernard Montgomery, against the Axis forces, commanded by German Field Marshal Erwin Rommel, also known as the "Desert Fox."

The stage for this pivotal clash was set in October 1942, near the small railway town of El Alamein in Egypt. The location was strategically significant; it stood as the gateway to the Suez Canal, a vital route for shipping and supplies. The Axis forces had pushed the Allies back, but the line held at El Alamein. If Rommel's troops could break through, they would have a clear path to the oil fields of the Middle East and potentially change the course of the war.

General Montgomery, aware of the high stakes, prepared his

troops meticulously for the confrontation. The Allied forces outnumbered the Axis troops, with a significant advantage in tanks and artillery. Montgomery's plan was to wear down the Axis forces with sustained artillery bombardments followed by a series of infantry attacks, slowly chipping away at their defenses.

The battle began on the night of October 23, 1942, with a massive artillery barrage that lit up the desert sky. Over 1,000 Allied guns fired upon Axis positions, signaling the start of a conflict that would last for nearly two weeks. The noise was deafening, and the ground shook under the relentless explosions. This initial assault was designed to weaken the Axis defenses and clear the way for infantry and tank units.

In the days that followed, the Allied forces launched a series of attacks against the Axis lines. The fighting was intense, with both sides enduring heavy losses. The desert landscape became a battleground marked by tank tracks and bomb craters, a testament to the ferocity of the conflict. Rommel, known for his tactical genius, maneuvered his forces skillfully, launching counterattacks that tested the resolve of the Allied troops.

Despite the challenges, the Allied forces, bolstered by their numerical superiority and air support, gradually gained ground. The supply situation for the Axis forces grew increasingly dire, as Allied control of the Mediterranean Sea made it difficult for Rommel to receive reinforcements and supplies.

After days of grueling combat, the tide began to turn in favor of the Allies. The Axis defenses were weakening, and Montgomery seized the opportunity to launch a decisive attack. On November 2, Allied forces broke through the Axis lines, forcing Rommel to order a retreat.

The Battle of El Alamein was a significant victory for the Allies. It marked the first major defeat of the Axis forces on land and was a turning point in the North African Campaign. The victory at El Alamein bolstered the morale of the Allied forces and proved to be a critical step toward the eventual defeat of the Axis powers in North Africa.

The story of El Alamein is not just about military tactics and desert warfare. It's a tale of determination, strategy, and the importance of resilience in the face of adversity. The battle demonstrated that even in the most challenging conditions, courage and careful planning could lead to success.

As the Battle of El Alamein progressed, the Allied forces, under General Montgomery, continued to apply pressure on the Axis forces. This phase of the battle demonstrated not only the strategic brilliance of the Allied command but also the courage and resilience of the soldiers who fought in the harsh desert environment.

In the days following the initial breakthrough, the Allied forces faced tough resistance from Axis troops, who fought desperately to hold their ground. The desert, with its vast, open spaces and lack of cover, made the battle particularly brutal. Soldiers had to contend not only with the enemy but also with the extreme conditions—blazing heat during the day and cold at night, along with sandstorms that could disorient even the most experienced troops.

A key factor in the Allies' success at El Alamein was their superior use of technology and intelligence. The Allies had cracked the codes used by the Axis to communicate, giving Montgomery and his staff invaluable insight into Rommel's plans and movements. This advantage allowed the Allies to anticipate and counter Axis attacks more effectively.

Furthermore, the Allies' superiority in air power proved decisive. The Royal Air Force (RAF) and the Allied air forces dominated the skies, providing crucial support to ground troops by targeting Axis tanks, supply lines, and troop positions. The ability to call in air strikes and reconnaissance flights gave the Allied forces a significant tactical advantage.

Amidst the strategy and technology, the human stories of El Alamein stand out. Soldiers from various countries and backgrounds came together to fight against a common enemy. Among them was Private James Thompson (a representative name), a young British soldier who found himself in the midst of his first major battle. Despite the fear and uncertainty, Thompson and his comrades pushed forward, motivated by a sense of duty and the camaraderie that developed among the troops.

The Axis forces, facing dwindling supplies and overwhelming odds, fought tenaciously. Rommel, aware of the strategic importance of El Alamein, made several attempts to break the Allied lines and relieve the pressure on his troops. However, the combined might of the Allied forces, coupled with their superior resources and intelligence, gradually wore down the Axis defenses.

As the battle entered its final stages, the determination of the Allied forces began to pay off. The Axis lines started to crumble under the continuous assault, and Rommel was forced to consider a retreat to save what remained of his army. The capture of key positions by the Allies made it increasingly difficult for the Axis to hold onto their territory.

The Battle of El Alamein was a showcase of military strategy, technological innovation, and human courage. It demonstrated the importance of unity among Allied forces and highlighted the contributions of individuals from diverse backgrounds to the common goal of defeating tyranny.

In the midst of the conflict, stories of individual bravery and sacrifice emerged. Soldiers like Private James Thompson, who had faced the horrors of war for the first time, became heroes in their own right. Each man's story was a testament to the resilience of the human spirit in the face of adversity. Across the battlefield, the camaraderie among the troops grew stronger, forging bonds that would last a lifetime.

Field Marshal Erwin Rommel, the legendary "Desert Fox," found himself in a difficult position. Known for his tactical genius, Rommel had led his troops through numerous victories. However, the situation at El Alamein was unlike any he had faced before. With his supply lines cut and his forces dwindling, Rommel made the difficult decision to order a strategic retreat. This move marked the beginning of the end for the Axis campaign in North Africa.

The retreat was a complex operation, carried out under the cover of darkness to avoid Allied air strikes. Despite their best efforts, the Axis forces suffered heavy losses during their withdrawal. The Allies, seizing the opportunity, pursued the retreating enemy, determined to capitalize on their advantage.

The victory at El Alamein had far-reaching consequences. It was not just a triumph on the battlefield; it was a symbol of hope for the Allied nations. News of the victory spread quickly, boosting morale among the troops and the civilian populations back home. For the first time since the start of the war, the defeat of the Axis powers seemed not just possible, but inevitable.

General Bernard Montgomery, the architect of the victory, became a national hero. His leadership and strategic acumen were widely celebrated. The success at El Alamein demonstrated the effectiveness of Allied cooperation and marked a turning point in the war. It paved the way for future operations, including the invasion of Italy and the eventual return to Western Europe.

As the dust settled over the North African desert, the significance of El Alamein became clear. It was a battle that had tested the limits of human endurance and military strategy. The lessons learned would inform future campaigns, and the stories of those who fought would be remembered for generations to come.

The Liberation of Paris and the victory at El Alamein were more than just military successes. They were milestones on the road to victory, symbols of what could be achieved when nations united against a common enemy. As we reflect on these events, we are reminded of the courage, determination, and solidarity that defined one of the most challenging periods in human history.

CHAPTER 12:
Animals in the War

Animals have played important roles in human conflicts throughout history, and World War II was no exception. From horses to homing pigeons, a variety of animals were called into service, performing tasks that were crucial to military operations and saving countless lives in the process.

One of the most celebrated animal heroes of World War II was a homing pigeon named G.I. Joe. This brave bird was tasked with delivering a critical message that saved the lives of more than 1,000 people. In October 1943, British forces planned to attack the Italian village of Calvi Vecchia, not knowing that the Germans had already retreated and that the villagers and British soldiers in the area would be in the line of fire. G.I. Joe flew 20 miles in just 20 minutes to deliver the message to call off the attack, just in time to prevent a tragedy.

Dogs also played a vital role in the war, serving as messengers, sentries, and even mine detectors. One remarkable dog was Chips, a German Shepherd-Husky-Collie mix, who served with the U.S. Army. Chips is best remembered for his actions during the invasion of Sicily, where he and his handler came under fire. Chips broke free, attacked an enemy machine-gun nest, and helped capture four soldiers. His bravery earned him a Silver Star and a Purple Heart, though these were later revoked due to a policy against awarding military decorations to animals. Despite this, Chips remained a hero in the eyes of those he served with.

Horses, though largely replaced by vehicles and machinery, still played a part in World War II. The Polish cavalry, for example, used horses in the early stages of the war. While the myth of Polish cavalry charging German tanks is just that—a myth—the horses were used for mobility and in areas where vehicles could not easily go.

Even more exotic animals found their way into the war effort. Elephants in India and Burma were used to move heavy objects and clear paths through dense jungles for troops, showcasing the versatility and importance of animals even in modern warfare.

These stories of animal heroes in World War II highlight the diverse ways in which bravery and loyalty are not just human traits but are found in the animal kingdom too. These animals, serving alongside human soldiers, made significant contributions to the war effort and saved lives through their actions. Their stories remind us of the bonds between humans and animals and the extraordinary ways in which animals have served in times of great need.

While exploring the remarkable contributions of animals during World War II, it becomes evident that their roles were as varied as they were vital. Beyond pigeons, dogs, and horses, many other animals served in unique capacities, each showcasing remarkable bravery and playing a pivotal role in both combat and non-combat situations.

Carrier pigeons, beyond G.I. Joe's notable contribution, were widely used across various theaters of war due to their reliability and speed. These birds were trained to fly long distances to deliver messages that could mean the difference between life and death. Another famous pigeon, named "The Mocker," flew 52 missions before being wounded. Pigeons' ability to return to their home lofts over long distances and in challenging conditions made them invaluable, especially in areas where modern communication was disrupted or unavailable.

Dogs' roles extended far beyond the battlefield. In addition to serving as sentries, messengers, and mine detectors, they also worked as search and rescue animals, helping to locate wounded soldiers after battles. Some dogs were trained as "paradogs," parachuting alongside airborne forces to provide immediate assistance upon landing. These dogs often carried medical supplies and messages and were trained to comfort injured soldiers as they waited for medical evacuation.

The story of Judy, a purebred English Pointer, highlights the resilience and loyalty of wartime animals. Judy served with the Royal Navy and was the only animal officially recognized as a prisoner of war during World War II. She provided companionship and protection to her fellow prisoners, alerting them to approaching enemies and dangerous animals, and helping to find water sources during their forced labor building the Sumatra Railway.

Horses and mules also played crucial roles, particularly in transporting supplies in areas where vehicles were impractical or unavailable. In the rugged terrain of the Italian and Burmese campaigns, mules carried food, water, ammunition, and medical supplies to front-line troops. Their endurance and ability to navigate difficult paths were indispensable to maintaining supply lines and ensuring that soldiers had the resources they needed to continue fighting.

Even camels and elephants were pressed into service. In the deserts of North Africa and the jungles of Burma, these animals performed tasks similar to those of horses and mules, showcasing the adaptability and importance of animals in warfare.

The contributions of these animals were not without cost. Many endured hardships similar to those faced by human soldiers, including injury, disease, and the stresses of combat. Their sacrifices were recognized by both their handlers and the military, with several animals receiving medals and honors for their bravery and service.

Through their diverse roles, animals in World War II demonstrated time and again their importance to the war effort. Their stories of courage, loyalty, and resilience serve as a reminder of the deep bonds between humans and animals and the extraordinary ways in which these bonds were forged in the crucible of war.

In examining the individual stories and contributions of animals during World War II, we uncover tales of extraordinary partnership and heroism that underscore the complexities of war and the universal spirit of resilience.

One such story is that of Bamse, a Saint Bernard who became a symbol of courage and loyalty. Bamse was the mascot of the Free Norwegian forces and served aboard a Norwegian Navy ship. He became famous for his remarkable deeds, including saving a crew member from drowning and stopping a knife fight simply by placing his paws on the combatants, showcasing not only his bravery but also his unique ability to protect and mediate in times of danger. Bamse's story illustrates the multifaceted roles animals played during the war, serving not only in combat roles but also providing emotional support and companionship to soldiers far from home.

Another notable animal hero was Smoky, a Yorkshire Terrier who served with American forces in the Pacific. Found by a soldier in a foxhole in New Guinea, Smoky went on to participate in numerous combat missions and survived over 150 air raids. Her most famous contribution was running a telegraph wire through a narrow, 70-foot pipe, saving soldiers days of dangerous work and exposure to enemy fire. Smoky's size and agility turned her into an unlikely hero, demonstrating that even the smallest animals could make significant contributions to the war effort.

These stories also highlight the deep bonds formed between

animals and their handlers, bonds forged in the adversity of war. Handlers relied on their animal companions not just for the tasks they performed but also for the comfort and sense of home they provided. In return, these animals were given unwavering loyalty, care, and respect, becoming integral members of their units.

The legacy of animals in World War II is not only in the medals or honors they received but in the lasting impact of their service on those they served with. After the war, many animals, like their human counterparts, were officially recognized for their bravery. Institutions like the Dickin Medal, often referred to as the "animal Victoria Cross," were established to honor the bravery and sacrifice of animals in conflict.

As we reflect on the contributions of animals to the Allied victory in World War II, we're reminded of the complexity of their roles and the profound effects they had on the human experience of war. Their stories are a testament to the enduring spirit of partnership between humans and animals, a reminder of the sacrifices made by all living beings in times of conflict, and a tribute to the extraordinary acts of courage that can emerge from the darkest times.

The tales of Bamse, Smoky, and countless others continue to inspire and teach us valuable lessons about bravery, loyalty, and the significant impact of the animal-human bond. These animals were not just mascots or tools of war; they were heroes in their own right, whose contributions were as varied as they were invaluable. As we move forward, their stories remain an integral part of our shared history, illustrating the universal capacity for heroism and the diverse forms it can take.

CHAPTER 13:

Douglas MacArthur: The Pacific's Protector

G eneral Douglas MacArthur was one of the most prominent military leaders of World War II, playing a key role in the Pacific theater. Known for his strategic brilliance and controversial personality, MacArthur's impact on the war's outcome in the Pacific was significant.

Born into a military family, MacArthur had a long and distinguished career in the U.S. Army before World War II. When the war broke out, he was in the Philippines, preparing its defenses against possible Japanese invasion. Despite his efforts, the Philippines fell to Japanese forces in 1942, leading to MacArthur's famous vow, "I shall return," as he was evacuated to Australia by order of President Franklin D. Roosevelt.

From Australia, MacArthur became Supreme Commander of Allied Forces in the Southwest Pacific Area. He began a series of island-hopping campaigns, bypassing heavily fortified Japanese positions to strike at more vulnerable locations. This strategy saved countless lives and resources, gradually turning the tide of the war in favor of the Allies.

One of MacArthur's most notable campaigns was the recapture of the Philippines in 1944. Fulfilling his promise to return, MacArthur's forces landed on Leyte Island, leading to a fierce battle that eventually resulted in the liberation of the Philippines. This victory was a critical step in cutting off Japan from its occupied territories in Southeast Asia and the Western Pacific, significantly weakening Japanese forces.

MacArthur's leadership style was unique; he was known for his ability to inspire his troops and his unshakeable confidence in victory. Despite facing criticism for some of his decisions, his strategic vision and determination were instrumental in the Allied forces' successes in the Pacific.

Douglas MacArthur's leadership in the Pacific Theater was marked by a series of strategic decisions that would have a lasting impact on the course of World War II. After the fall of the Philippines and his subsequent retreat to Australia, MacArthur was determined to strike back against the Japanese forces. His approach to warfare in the Pacific was characterized by a strategic innovation known as "island hopping," which involved bypassing heavily fortified Japanese positions to attack weaker spots, thereby cutting supply lines and isolating key enemy bases.

One of the pivotal moments in MacArthur's campaign was the

Battle of Leyte Gulf in the Philippines. This battle was one of the largest naval battles in history and was crucial for the recapture of the Philippines. MacArthur's promise to return to the Philippines was fulfilled when he waded ashore at Leyte in October 1944, a moment captured in an iconic photograph that symbolized hope and imminent victory to the Allied forces and the Filipino people. The battle that ensued was fierce, with both sides suffering heavy losses. However, the strategic brilliance of the Allied forces, coupled with MacArthur's leadership, ultimately led to a decisive victory that severely weakened the Japanese Navy and paved the way for further Allied advances in the region.

MacArthur's strategy in the Pacific was not without its critics. Some argued that his approach was too cautious and that it prolonged the war unnecessarily. However, MacArthur was deeply committed to minimizing casualties among his troops and believed that his strategy of island hopping was the most effective way to achieve victory without unnecessary loss of life. His attention to the welfare of his soldiers earned him deep respect and loyalty from those he commanded.

In addition to his military strategy, MacArthur was also known for his efforts to rebuild and rehabilitate the territories liberated from Japanese control. In Japan, following the war's end, he oversaw the occupation and played a significant role in reforming Japanese society, laying the foundations for the democratic and peaceful Japan that exists today. His work in Japan demonstrated his belief in the importance of not just winning the war, but also in ensuring a lasting peace.

Through his campaigns in the Pacific, General Douglas MacArthur emerged as a figure larger than life, embodying the complexities and contradictions of military leadership in times of war. His strategic genius, coupled with his flair for the dramatic, left an indelible mark on the history of World War II.

General Douglas MacArthur's approach to the Pacific campaign was underscored by his determination to avoid direct assaults on the most fortified Japanese positions whenever possible. This strategy not only preserved the lives of Allied soldiers but also allowed for a more efficient advance toward Japan. MacArthur's island-hopping strategy was evident in operations such as the battles for New Guinea, which became a series of engagements that gradually pushed the Japanese forces back and cut off their supply lines, severely limiting their ability to sustain their defensive positions.

MacArthur's leadership was not just strategic but also deeply personal. He was known for his commitment to his soldiers' welfare, often visiting front-line positions and medical facilities to offer encouragement and support. His public vow to return to the Philippines became a rallying cry for the Filipino people and the Allied forces in the Pacific, symbolizing hope and the unwavering commitment to victory against Japan.

The liberation of the Philippines, culminating in the Battle of Leyte Gulf, was a turning point in the Pacific War. The successful execution of this campaign highlighted MacArthur's strategic foresight and his ability to conduct large-scale amphibious operations. The recapture of the Philippines effectively cut Japan off from its occupied territories in Southeast Asia, crippling its ability to resupply and reinforcing the inevitability of Allied victory.

Following the war, MacArthur's role in overseeing the occupation of Japan showcased his understanding of the importance of rebuilding and reconciliation in the aftermath of conflict. His administration implemented significant reforms, including the drafting of a new constitution that transformed Japan into a democratic nation. MacArthur's efforts in post-war Japan exemplified his belief in the potential for change and the importance of establishing a foundation for lasting peace.

As we reflect on General MacArthur's contributions to the Allied victory in the Pacific, we can appreciate the complexity of military leadership and the strategic decisions that can alter the course of history. MacArthur's legacy is a testament to the impact one individual can have on the outcome of global events, highlighting themes of courage, innovation, and the pursuit of peace after the devastation of war.

MacArthur's island-hopping strategy not only exemplified military ingenuity but also showcased a profound commitment to preserving the lives of his soldiers and minimizing civilian casualties. This approach, while criticized by some for its cautious nature, ultimately proved to be one of the key factors leading to the successful conclusion of the Pacific campaign. The recapture of the Philippines, a promise MacArthur made and famously kept, stands as a pivotal moment in the war, symbolizing hope and the unwavering resolve of the Allied forces.

Beyond the battlefield, MacArthur's vision for a post-war Asia reshaped the political landscape of the region. His administration in Japan laid down the foundations for what would become a vibrant democracy, highlighting his ability to see beyond military conquest to the importance of building peace and stability in the aftermath of war. His reforms in Japan have had a lasting impact, contributing to the country's recovery and its emergence as a peaceful nation dedicated to democratic principles.

MacArthur's legacy is multifaceted, reflecting the complexities of war and the challenges of leadership. MacArthur's story exemplifies not just the tactical brilliance required in warfare but also the vision needed to secure a lasting peace. His actions remind us of the importance of strategic thinking, the value of perseverance in the face of adversity, and the profound effects of compassionate leadership on the world stage.

We're left with enduring lessons about the nature of leadership, the intricacies of military strategy, and the transformative power of visionary post-conflict reconstruction. MacArthur's contributions to the Allied victory in the Pacific and his role in shaping the post-war era continue to be studied and admired, offering insights into the complexities of historical events and the individuals who shape them.

CHAPTER 14:

Guadalcanal: The Fight for the Pacific Islands

The Battle of Guadalcanal was a pivotal moment in World War II, marking the first major offensive by Allied forces against the Empire of Japan. Located in the Solomon Islands, Guadalcanal became the scene of intense fighting between American and Japanese forces, lasting from August 1942 to February 1943. This battle was not just about controlling a piece of land; it was about gaining the upper hand in the Pacific Theater and stopping the advance of Japanese forces.

American troops, known as Marines, landed on Guadalcanal on August 7, 1942, with the goal of capturing an airfield that the Japanese were building on the island. This airfield, later named Henderson Field, was crucial because it could control sea routes around the Solomon Islands and threaten Allied movements in the Pacific. The Marines' surprise landing caught the Japanese defenders off guard, allowing the Americans to quickly secure the airfield.

However, taking the airfield was one thing; holding it was another. The Japanese launched several attempts to retake Henderson Field, leading to fierce battles in the air, on land, and at sea. Nighttime naval battles in the waters around Guadalcanal were particularly brutal and costly for both sides. One such battle, the Battle of Savo Island, resulted in significant losses for the Allies but did not deter them from their mission.

On land, the jungle environment of Guadalcanal posed a daunting challenge to both American and Japanese soldiers. Malaria, malnutrition, and the harsh conditions took a toll, making the fight for Guadalcanal as much a battle against the elements as against the enemy. Soldiers faced not only the well-entrenched Japanese forces but also had to contend with crocodiles, mosquitoes, and dense vegetation that made every advance difficult.

Despite these challenges, the determination and resilience of the American forces, supported by their allies, gradually turned the tide of the battle. The struggle for Guadalcanal showcased the importance of teamwork, strategy, and perseverance under the most difficult conditions.

The Battle of Guadalcanal stands out in history not just for its strategic significance but also for the extraordinary stories of courage and determination exhibited by those who fought. After seizing the airfield, which they renamed Henderson Field,

American forces quickly set to work fortifying their positions. The Japanese, recognizing the threat the captured airfield posed to their dominance in the Pacific, were determined to reclaim it at all costs.

The ensuing battles were marked by a series of intense, close-quarters engagements, both on the land and at sea. The jungle terrain of Guadalcanal proved to be a formidable challenge for both sides. American and Japanese soldiers had to deal not only with each other but also with the dense foliage that reduced visibility, the relentless rain that turned paths into mud, and the myriad of tropical diseases that sapped their strength.

Naval battles played a crucial role in the campaign. The waters around the Solomon Islands became known as "Ironbottom Sound," due to the number of ships sunk there from both sides. One of the most notable naval clashes was the Battle of Guadalcanal in November 1942, a complex engagement that spanned several days and involved dozens of ships and aircraft from both the American and Japanese fleets. Despite suffering heavy losses, the American navy managed to prevent the Japanese from landing significant reinforcements on the island, thereby securing a strategic advantage.

On land, one of the most heroic figures of the campaign was Sergeant John Basilone of the United States Marine Corps. Basilone's bravery during the Battle for Henderson Field, where he manned a machine gun post under heavy fire to hold off a Japanese attack, earned him the Medal of Honor. His actions exemplified the grit and determination of the American forces stationed on

Guadalcanal.

The struggle for control of the island also highlighted the importance of air power. The "Cactus Air Force," a name given to the Allied air units based at Henderson Field, played a pivotal role in defending the airfield from Japanese air and ground attacks. Despite being outnumbered and often outgunned, these pilots managed to inflict significant damage on Japanese ships and aircraft, proving the value of air superiority in modern warfare.

The battle for Guadalcanal was a brutal campaign that tested the limits of human endurance. It was a fight not just for control of a strategic point but for survival in some of the harshest conditions imaginable. The victory at Guadalcanal marked the beginning of the end of Japanese expansion in the Pacific, proving that the Allied forces could not only stop the Japanese advance but also turn the tide of the war.

The Battle of Guadalcanal was not only a testament to the strategic and tactical ingenuity of the Allied forces but also a stark reminder of the harsh realities of war. The campaign showcased the significance of intelligence, logistics, and the human spirit in overcoming adversity. As the battle progressed, both sides faced immense challenges, from the logistical nightmare of supplying troops over vast distances to the psychological strain of continuous combat in punishing conditions.

The resolve of the Allied forces, particularly the Marines and the Army units that took part in the campaign, was put to the test as they encountered fierce resistance from the Japanese. The determination to hold Henderson Field against repeated assaults became a defining characteristic of the Allied effort on Guadalcanal. This resolve was mirrored in the air and at sea, where Allied naval and air forces engaged in a relentless struggle to cut off Japanese reinforcements and supplies.

The turning point of the campaign came with the successful defense of Henderson Field and the increasing difficulty faced by the Japanese in resupplying their garrison on the island. The Allied strategy of interdiction, which targeted Japanese supply ships, began to take its toll, slowly strangling the Japanese forces' ability to sustain their offensive capabilities. This, combined with the relentless pressure applied by ground forces, eventually led to the decision by Japanese command to withdraw their troops, marking a significant strategic victory for the Allies.

The aftermath of the Battle of Guadalcanal highlighted the importance of combined arms operations and the need for effective coordination between land, air, and sea forces. It also underscored the value of intelligence in shaping operational decisions and the critical role of logistics in sustaining military campaigns. The lessons learned from Guadalcanal would inform Allied strategy in the Pacific for the remainder of the war, contributing to the eventual defeat of Japan.

Exploring the end of the Battle of Guadalcanal and its wider implications offers valuable lessons on resilience, strategy, and the human cost of war. As the Allied forces celebrated their hard-earned victory, the significance of their triumph extended far beyond the confines of the island. Guadalcanal became a turning point in the Pacific Theater, demonstrating that the Japanese advance could be stopped and reversed.

The battle's conclusion in early 1943 marked the first major Allied land victory against Japan, setting the stage for further operations across the Pacific. The success at Guadalcanal bolstered Allied morale and proved the effectiveness of joint operations, where air, land, and naval forces worked in concert to achieve a common goal. This victory also emphasized the importance of perseverance; despite initial setbacks and the daunting challenges posed by the environment and the well-entrenched enemy, the Allied forces adapted and overcame.

The campaign's aftermath also highlighted the cost of warfare. Both sides suffered significant losses, with thousands of soldiers, sailors, and airmen making the ultimate sacrifice. The island itself bore the scars of battle, serving as a somber reminder of the conflict's intensity. The resilience of those who fought, their dedication to the mission, and their ability to endure in the face of adversity are central to the legacy of Guadalcanal.

For the soldiers who survived, the battle was a defining experience, shaping their understanding of warfare and comradeship. The stories of individual bravery, strategic ingenuity, and unwavering commitment to the cause of freedom continue to inspire and educate. Through these stories, we can learn about the complexities of historical conflicts, the value of teamwork, and the indomitable spirit required to face and overcome challenges.

The campaign exemplifies how determination, strategic planning, and the courage of individuals can influence the course of history. It reminds us of the sacrifices made in the pursuit of peace and security and the importance of remembering those who served and sacrificed in times of global conflict.

The Battle of Guadalcanal stands as a testament to the complexities of war and the human capacity for resilience and heroism. It's a chapter of World War II that not only shaped the outcome of the conflict but also offers enduring lessons on courage, sacrifice, and the importance of standing up against adversity.

CHAPTER 15:
The Four Chaplains' Sacrifice

The story of the Four Chaplains is a remarkable tale of bravery, selflessness, and interfaith camaraderie during World War II, highlighting the profound acts of heroism that can emerge in the darkest times. This story begins on the USAT Dorchester, a United States Army transport ship that was part of a convoy headed to Greenland during the war.

Onboard the Dorchester were four chaplains: George Fox, a Methodist; Alexander Goode, a Jewish rabbi; Clark Poling, a Dutch Reformed minister; and John Washington, a Roman Catholic priest. Despite their different faiths, the chaplains shared a common bond of spiritual commitment and a deep sense of duty to the men serving alongside them.

The Dorchester was navigating the treacherous waters of the North Atlantic on February 3, 1943, when disaster struck. A German submarine, U-223, spotted the convoy and launched a torpedo that struck the Dorchester, causing severe damage and panic among the crew and passengers. As the ship began to sink into the icy waters, chaos ensued.

Amidst the confusion and fear, the Four Chaplains sprang into action. They calmed frightened soldiers, guided the wounded to safety, and distributed life jackets. When the supply of life jackets ran out, the chaplains made the ultimate sacrifice: they removed their own life jackets and gave them to soldiers who had none.

In the final moments before the Dorchester sank, survivors witnessed an unforgettable scene: the Four Chaplains, arms linked, praying together and singing hymns as they willingly gave up their chances of survival to save others. Their selfless act of bravery and faith in the face of certain death has become an enduring symbol of the transcendent power of self-sacrifice and unity.

The legacy of the Four Chaplains serves as a powerful example of how individuals from different backgrounds and faiths can come together in solidarity to make a profound difference in the lives of others. Their story is not just a testament to their courage but also a reminder of the values of compassion, sacrifice, and interfaith harmony.

Before the tragedy, the chaplains had become friends, their bonds forged by shared service and a common goal to provide spiritual support to the soldiers. Their interfaith collaboration was a testament to their belief in universal values of faith, courage, and compassion. They held services together, prayed together, and were there for every soldier, regardless of religious background.

In the chaos following the torpedo hit, as soldiers scrambled for lifeboats and safety, the chaplains' presence was a calming force. They helped organize an orderly evacuation, offered prayers, and provided comfort to those in despair. Their actions went beyond the call of duty, focusing on the well-being of the soldiers rather than their own safety.

When it became evident that there were not enough life jackets for everyone, the chaplains made a decision that would immortalize them in history. Without hesitation, they gave their own life jackets to four young men, knowing full well that this act meant certain death in the freezing waters. Witnesses reported seeing the chaplains standing arm in arm, praying and singing hymns as the ship went down. Their selflessness in those final moments was a profound act of faith and humanity.

The sacrifice of the Four Chaplains became a symbol of extraordinary selflessness and interfaith harmony. It showed that in the face of death, compassion and unity could prevail over despair and division. The story of their sacrifice spread quickly, inspiring a nation at war and becoming a lasting legacy of bravery, sacrifice, and unity.

Their legacy is remembered and honored in various ways. In 1948, the U.S. Postal Service issued a commemorative stamp in their honor, a rare recognition for individuals who had not been presidents or military generals. The Chaplains' Medal for Heroism was posthumously awarded to them in 1961, and numerous memorials and foundations have been established to continue their mission of unity and interfaith understanding.

In the wake of the Four Chaplains' sacrifice, communities and individuals across the United States and beyond were moved by their story. It wasn't just the act of giving up their life jackets that captured the public's imagination; it was the unity and mutual respect among the chaplains from different faith backgrounds. Their collective decision to face fate together, without regard to religious differences, stands as a powerful example of interfaith harmony and mutual support.

This spirit of inclusivity and mutual respect sparked conversations about tolerance, understanding, and cooperation among diverse groups. Schools, civic organizations, and religious groups have used the story of the Four Chaplains as a teaching moment to highlight the importance of coming together for the common good, especially in times of crisis or conflict.

Moreover, the chaplains' story has been commemorated in various ways, emphasizing different aspects of their legacy. Monuments and memorials dedicated to their memory can be found in chapels, public parks, and cemeteries across the country, each serving as a focal point for community reflection on the values they embodied. Annual ceremonies and services are held to honor their memory, often focusing on themes of sacrifice, service, and unity.

In educational settings, the story of the Four Chaplains is used to teach not only history but also ethics and character education. It serves as a profound example of moral courage and the impact of ethical leadership. Teachers and educators draw on their story to inspire students to think about how they can demonstrate similar values in their own lives, encouraging acts of kindness, empathy, and cooperation among peers.

As we continue to explore the significance of the Four Chaplains' sacrifice, it becomes evident that their legacy is not confined to the historical events of World War II but resonates with timeless lessons on human dignity, sacrifice for others, and the strength that comes from unity. Their story reminds us that even in moments of great adversity, there is an opportunity to demonstrate the best of what it means to be human.

The Four Chaplains' sacrifice is a testament to the power of selfless action and the enduring impact such actions can have on society. It encourages us to consider how we, too, can embody the values of courage, sacrifice, and unity in our daily lives, fostering a more compassionate and understanding world.

Made in the USA
Columbia, SC
19 December 2024

50123121R00059